Meet the HENRYs

Meet the HENRYs

The Millennials that Matter Most for Luxury Brands

Pamela N. Danziger

Paramount Market Publishing, Inc.

Paramount Market Publishing, Inc.
274 North Goodman Street, STE D-214
Rochester, NY 14607
www.paramountbooks.com
607-275-8100

Publisher: James Madden

Editorial Director: Doris Walsh

Printed in USA

Cataloging in Publication Data available

ISBN-13: 978-1-941688-58-8 *paper*

eISBN-13: 978-1-941688-59-5

Dedication

For my next-generation HENRYs
Genevieve and Ariel
and soon-to-be
Nathanael

Contents

HENRYs and the Brands They Love

Introduction

A brand "bromance" is brewing in the luxury market between new e-commerce-driven companies that Marvin Traub Associates calls the "New Davids" and the affluent young HENRYs (high-earners-not-rich-yet).

The TRAUB report defines the "New Davids"as:

> Over 200 brands across five key categories: fashion, accessories, beauty, wellness and home. By definition, our Davids were founded, launched and nurtured online and our curation is centered on those which we believe are ones to watch.

These disruptive 200 "New Davids" brands attract the attention and loyalty of the next generation of luxury consumers, the young HENRYs. These customers have high income now, but even higher projected incomes for the future. This gives them discretion and willingness to spend on brands that talk their language and meet their lifestyle needs. HENRYs love the "New Davids," and it's sure to be a long-term romance.

"New Davids" are new luxury brands HENRYs love

Mortimer Singer, Chief Executive Officer of TRAUB, credits the launch of **Bonobos** in 2007 with triggering his company's consciousness of the "New Davids" trend. Bonobos is a prime example of the new luxury brands that HENRYs love, offering fashion-forward styling, high quality at accessible prices. Notably, Bonobos is now a Walmart brand, acquired for $310 million in 2017.

The young HENRYs are finding spirituality through spending, or the 'laying on of hands' to brands that resonate with their values.

"Bonobos was a seminal moment in this shift into a new era of the 'I-brand,'" Singer says. "It's about the consumer 'laying on of hands' to a brand. The customer becomes part of an extended tribe of people bound together by the brand. The 'New Davids' brands are forging the future of retail in this HENRY millennial world."

His allusion to the almost religious fervor that HENRYs feel for the "New Davids" reflects today's young affluents who are searching for deeper meaning in their lives. That includes how they express themselves as consumers.

"It's the notion that in the world the younger generation lives in, they are more connected through technology, but not necessarily in the physical world," Singer explains. "They have a deep need for spirituality, yet they aren't necessarily turning to organized religion to fulfill that need."

"The young HENRYs are finding spirituality through spending, or the 'laying on of hands' to brands that resonate with their values, like how they treat the environment, their employees, and the animals they source their products from on a 360° basis of sustainability," Singer affirms.

That said, as these "New David" businesses grow, will they lose their "religion?" "The studies would suggest that these young values-focused companies may lose some of those founding ideals as they mature," Singer predicts.

"Most of these brands are quite small individually, though if you put all 200 companies together, they are doing about $1 billion in America," he says.

"Many of them would be happy to build a $100 million business that is profitable and self-sustaining. But other entrepreneurs will feel the need to chase revenue and so will turn to venture capital which will demand growth. That is why many of these companies are now putting down brick-and-mortar roots to deliver new experiences," he continues.

CASE STUDY: Naadam

How Naadam connects with HENRYs' lifestyle aspirations

Singer is impressed with one noteworthy "New David" called **Naadam**, a brand devoted to offering the finest quality cashmere at an affordable price. Its tag line: Ethical Luxury For The Way We Want To Live. Its story connects with the HENRYs' lifestyle aspirations, offering products that fit their fashion profile at prices they can afford today.

"Naadam means celebration in Mongolian," Singer explains. Having tired of their day jobs, company founders, Matt Scanlan working in venture capital and Diederik Rijsemus in econometrics, set out on motorcycles through the Gobi Desert, where they bought up as much of the best cashmere they could find from the herders they met.

They brought it back to a 140-year-old family-run mill in the Italian Alps to be spun into yarn. "Today they are doing an incredible business, based on the idea you don't have to spend $500 for great quality cashmere," says Singer.

Naadam represents a new kind of 21st-century vertically integrated business model because the company is putting money back into creating a sustainable cashmere ecosystem.

The company has established a privately-funded non-profit that provides veterinary programs, livestock insurance, and breeding development. In return, Naadam is granted first access to the herders' fleece, according to the company website.

This business model stretches from the slopes of Mongolia to American HENRYs' closets, and breeds a deep connection with the customer: "Naadam tells the story to consumers so they feel like they are on a Mongolian farm," Singer says. "It transports the customers on a journey. Naadam sells $250 sweaters along with a yarn business, and has recently launched a line into department stores called Naadam Studios."

"Naadam has learned from the 20th-century business playbook but applies the top spin of 21st-century rules. These young entrepreneurs are respectful of those who have gone before them, but they are not scared to challenge the playbook. It's a fully integrated business model that goes from farm to closet to complete the circle," Singer explains.

Advice for "Goliaths" to think like and act like "New Davids"

Even though the companies that the TRAUB study identified have modest revenues today, the retail "Goliaths" still have much to learn from the "New Davids."

"The 'New Davids' are the smoke of where the fire is," Singer shares. "They reflect the shift in how consumers are spending their money, on experiences, dining, travel, electronics, video, technology, much that is outside the traditional boundaries of retail," he says.

"The problem is, people tend to think the 'New Davids' are too small and not really worth investing in or acquiring until they are profitable or bigger. But if some big companies would acquire one of these emerging companies, it could make them profitable the next day through the huge back-office support they could offer," Singer explains.

He points to **Nordstrom** as being a pioneer in investing in "New David" companies with new ideas of what luxury is and who it is for, having recently acquired **Trunk Club** and direct-to-consumer shoe company **Sole Society**, as well as partnering with **BaubleBar** to sell fashion jewelry in its stores. Why? "It's a smart thing to do in order to get to know this customer better," Singer says.

The 'New Davids' shook the cage in the luxury market. We needed it.

"The notion that the internet is going to kill full-price retail is misguided and just plain wrong," Singer notes. "The 'New Davids' are showing how to create deep connections with the younger generation. Through them, the 'Goliath' department stores can learn how to get better and more powerful. The 'Goliaths' need to embrace new ways to activate shoppers in the stores."

"The 'New Davids' shook the cage in the luxury market. We needed it," Singer concludes. "And the millennial HENRYs after the recession fueled it. It means established companies have to align themselves differently and shift focus to give the retail industry renewed vigor. There is a huge opportunity waiting for them if they do."

"New Davids" Are Challenging the Establishment

Traditional, long-established retailers feel much like sitting ducks today. While the National Retail Federation tries to encourage the industry with Vice President Pence playing cheerleader at a recent NRF Retail Advocacy Summit saying, "The best days for American retailers are ahead," most of those in the audience must have agreed, simply because retail seems so bad now.

In just the first half of 2018, retailers fell in record numbers: 8,640 will close shop, according to a recent Credit Suisse report. The current closure rate is 40 percent higher than at its 2008 peak when 6,200 were shuttered. Further, Credit Suisse predicts that 275 malls, 25 percent of the nation's 1,200 total, will close within the next five short years.

NRF president Matthew Shay can "push back on the apocalyptic narrative," but if he got down off the stage and out into the stores and the malls, he couldn't ignore the obvious: Retailers have been slow, way too slow, to respond to the shifting patterns and preferences of American shoppers, most especially the HENRYs.

Amazon continues unabated to siphon dollars out of the malls and stores. It's become so bad that "being Amazoned" has now entered the business lexicon.

While prospects look poor for traditional retail, there is still plenty of capital ready to invest in the right opportunity. Robin Lewis, founder and CEO of *The Robin Report* and co-author of the book, *The New Rules of Retail,* says, "Some $2 trillion of corporate capital remains sidelined because businesses don't see enough of an increase in consumer demand to justify investing that capital in growth." But nobody is going to throw good money after bad to prop up failing traditional retail strategies.

Recent mergers and acquisitions, notably **Walmart**'s acquisition of digitally-native **Jet.com**, **ModCloth**, and **Bonobos**, point to a way for traditional retailers to pull themselves out of the abyss.

Retailers must apply new-age thinking to solve 21st-century retailing challenges and that requires bold and aggressive moves, not reworking of stale, outmoded strategies.

Innovation is needed now

Retail innovation is desperately needed now. Fortunately, Dave Knox, who heads up Brandery, has written the guide book for that in *Predicting the Turn: The High Stakes Game of Business Between Startups and Blue Chips.* It is not too late for traditional retailers to get out ahead of consumers and respond to their needs.

Knox sees that the way forward for traditional retailers is to redefine the business they are in and invest accordingly. It's not just "selling more stuff to more people more often," as marketing strategist Sergio Zyman said, but anticipating consumer needs and being able to deliver proactively in the fastest, easiest, most efficient ways possible.

That means breaking out of old habits of basing

strategies on past performance and backward-looking indicators and replacing them with proactive, anticipatory thinking that looks ahead to the next turn. Next generation HENRYs are the bellwether of that turn.

Retailers need to invest not just in acquiring new brands and new tools, but more importantly in human capital that has this new way of predictive thinking programmed into its DNA. For such retail investment, Knox notes, "There is a lot of value besides just the financial returns."

Next generation HENRYs are the bellwether of the next turn.

Knox knows what he is talking about, being groomed in traditional CPG strategies through a seven-year stint with Procter & Gamble, all the while working on the side with innovative startups and advising venture funds.

How to get ready for the turn

A lot has been written about the disruptive change in business, but Knox's book takes you behind the scenes to give businesses tools to deal proactively with it.

"I saw this need for these two worlds to understand each other and also to wake up the big companies in particular, that the game of business has really changed. They needed to understand that the competition that was going to change their business wasn't necessarily going to be that which is directly in front of them," he says.

For many inbred, deeply ingrained reasons, the disruptive change that causes the turn most often doesn't come from the boardrooms of the Blue Chips, but from startups with the innovative thinking on which they are founded. They identify problems invisible to Blue Chips and find opportunities in the Blue Chips' corporate blindness.

Knox sees that the big innovation opportunity for retail Blue Chips, like **Walmart**, **Target**, **Macy's**, **Kroger**, and others, is to invest in startups, since organically-grown innovation is frequently discouraged by Wall Street and the investment community with its focus on quarterly returns.

The "New Davids" are the canary in the coal mine

"Historically companies look at the individual competitor, but often times miss the societal shift that is the indicator coming out of it," Knox explains. "They need to think about these players not just as a brand to acquire, but how they can bring a business model and a way of doing business that they fundamentally don't have."

In retail, the best and brightest startups have been born and bred on the internet and TRUAB's "New Davids" are the pick list of retail startups where traditional retailers can find new ideas and new blood.

On the "New Davids," Knox says, "I view all of the Davids as the canary in the coal mine. They are the indicator of change." To explain, he points to **Dollar Shave**

Club and its subscription-commerce model as a big turn in the traditional CPG world, which is optimized around shipping truckloads full of merchandise out to retailers' distribution warehouses. Customers on the other hand want delivery of individual packages to their homes in anticipation of their needs. In a prescient move, Blue Chip Unilever acquired Dollar Shave Club in 2016 and bought not just the brand, but the subscription-model expertise along with it.

"A lot of big companies looked at who was doing subscription commerce in their space and made the assessment of whether that company was a threat or not. They ignored the fact that there was $300 million invested in subscription commerce across the board. That was an indicator of a business model change. They should have been looking at the business model change, not the individual companies as a competitor," Knox says.

Traditional retailers need transformational innovation

Knox explains that corporate innovation arises in three ways:

- **Core innovation** which is focused on increasing market share in the business you are already in;
- **Adjacent innovation** which is one degree of separation into adjacencies, like Starbucks going into packaged coffee for the home; and
- **Transformation innovation** which is a complete

reworking of the business model and into a new category. Knox points to Amazon and its cloud computing Amazon Web Services, which, he says, "shares synergies with its core business but is something totally new."

It is the latter transformational innovation that retailers need now because that is where the big opportunities lie. "In terms of Blue Chip investment, it typically breaks down to 70 percent in core, 20 percent in adjacencies, and 10 percent in transformation," Knox says. "But the returns are flipped, 70 percent through transformation, 20 percent through adjacencies and only 10 percent in core."

To their detriment, too many retailers have been investing only on adjacency and core innovation, trying to fix problems in small incremental steps, not in transformational innovation that is needed. "Over the past 10-15 years, people have been intimidated to do transformative innovation. They have been forced to focus on their core business and not get distracted," Knox says.

Blue Chip retailers can modestly invest in transformational start-ups, like Walmart did with Bonobos, in order to get huge returns. "You are placing a lot of bets, but the one that works is going to work big," Knox advises.

But even more importantly, those transformational investments can mean the retail business is positioned for the next turn. And by acquiring new talent that has mastered the new business models, traditional retailers have a totally new perspective to predict what's next and get ahead of it, not be swallowed by it.

Meet the HENRYS

Think Young

The Wall Street Journal recently reported that 26-year-olds are the customers that retailers are most eager to attract. Why? Because they are the single biggest age cohort in the American population today, numbering 4.8 million. Those aged 26 are smack dab in the middle of the millennial generation, "the group of 93 million comprises people born roughly between 1980 and 2000," *The Journal* writes. By comparison, baby boomers, born from 1946 to 1964 and numbering 78.8 million at their peak, have now declined to 74 million according to the latest census.

Millennials, aged 18-38, are vital to every brands' future, as they are entering prime spending years buying homes and making improvements. Their outlays are growing as more of the generation moves into adulthood. Their importance will only continue to grow until about age 50 when their household spending is expected to peak, according to spending wave research conducted by Harry Dent. That means from now until about 2040, millennials will be the key consumer segment driving the U.S. economy.

The *WSJ* article is filled with valuable data and interesting anecdotes about how different the millennials are from previous generations, especially their baby boomer parents. As a result, "companies are developing new products, overhauling marketing, and launching educational programs – all with the goal of luring the archetypal 26-year-old," the article reports.

But amid the data reported, one critical perspective is missing: 26-year-olds' income. Yes, age of the customer is important in targeting the things they will buy, but even more important for marketers is to understand their spending potential. At any age, those customers with the highest income spend two-to-three times more in any category than those in the middle. So retailers need to focus not just on the consumers' age but also on their income to tap the 26-year-old's lifetime spending potential.

Millennials ahead of 75 percent of the rest of the country are prime – The HENRYs

The 26-year-old millennials on the road to affluence, called HENRYs (High-Earners-Not-Rich-Yet), are the customers whom retailers really need to zoom in on. That would be the 20 to 25 percent of those 4.8 million 26-year-olds who are at the top of the income distribution, or the 1.2 million earning more than 75 to 80 percent of their peers.

According to personal financial site DQYDJ's income calculator, the 26-year-olds earning just over $50,000 are at the head of the pack in earnings, with the average income of 26-year-olds being about $32,500. At $55,000, a 26-year-old crosses over into the top 20 percent of their age group, and at $75,000 they break into the top 10 percent. However, few at that age have reached incomes of $100,000, the line that defines HENRYs. It will take a few more years before they reach that threshold, but they are coming.

Young HENRYs are likely to out-earn their peers throughout their adulthood.

These 26-year-olds at the top 10 percent of their age group, earning so much more than their peers, are not only at the forefront of income; they are more educated, are more informed and, given their leadership among this age group, are setting the trends that those at lower incomes will follow.

And since they are making so much more money at such a young age, they are likely to continue to out-earn their peers throughout their adulthood. Marketers that really want to get a bead on the 26-year-olds so critical to their future should focus attention on the high-earners at the vanguard of the pack – the HENRYs earning $100,000 or more.

What do 26-year-old HENRYs want?

In researching any consumer market segment, just as in detective fiction and police investigations, you need three perspectives:

- **Means** – Who can afford what you are selling?
- **Opportunity** – Consumers' past purchase behavior often predicts their future behavior;
- **Motive** – Who has the need, who has the desire?

Let's dig further:

Means describes demographics of HENRYs

The demographic characteristics of the HENRY market segment are the place to start. With age (26) and income ($100,000-plus) as the baseline, these young HENRYs are also likely to share other defining demographics.

For example, high levels of education put people on the path of affluence and certain career paths, e.g., technology, business, finance, engineering, healthcare, are more promising to yield high incomes than others. HENRYs are more likely be to married and live a more traditional lifestyle with a focus on financial planning and a long-term perspective, rather than a "live fast, die young" approach. They are also likely to own homes now or plan to shortly.

Opportunity describes HENRYs' purchase behavior

As we know, past behavior tends to predict future behavior, so marketers want to make their brand a "habit" when consumers are young to carry forward their connection into the future. While there is much conjecture about whether millennials are brand loyal in the same way their parents' generation was, brand habits established at a young age save consumers the trouble of researching, testing, and trial that connecting with a new brand requires.

It's the strategy behind **Amazon PRIME**, **Costco**, **Blue Apron**, **Dollar Shave Club**, **Trunk Club**, **Stitch Fix** and so many emerging membership brands. It's the power of inertia, where people that opt-in are more likely to stay in, that is part of the Nudge Theory that helped win behavioral scientist Richard Thaler the Nobel Prize in Economics in 2018. If a brand can become embedded into millennials' lifestyle when they are young, it can become a brand for life.

The marketing opportunity is also defined by lifestage. The young HENRYs with an eye toward the future are in the market for fashions that project their professional goals and the dress standards of their professional colleagues. This has given rise to a whole influx of new-age fashion brands to fill the bill, like **Everlane**, **SuitSupply**, **Madewell**, **Free People**, and **Bonobos**.

At this life stage they are making or will shortly make home operations and furnishings purchases, as the *WSJ* highlights with how **P&G** is poised to target "new movers" among this cohort with the household supplies they will need setting up home, such as Swiffer duster, Mr. Clean Magic Eraser, and Tide detergent pods.

West Elm offers service packages to provide plumbing,

electrical, painting and art/mirror hanging services along with furniture offerings sized right for millennial's smaller-scale homes; **Home Depot** has been establishing its stores as education centers to teach millennials DIY home basics; and **JCPenney** is re-entering the home appliance market with models aimed at millennials' tastes.

Motive is the underlying consumer psychology

Among the three perspectives, understanding the consumers' motive to buy is the most important of all three perspectives. Unlike purchase behavior and brand preferences, which can change on a dime, consumers' underlying psychology is their set point. It characterizes their basic consumer motivations regardless of how other factors change. This is the psychographics or psychology of the customers and target customers.

Marketers must combine strategies from high-end brands, along with mass-market tactics.

Spend-thrift consumers tend to always be spendthrifts unless they make concerted efforts to change their behavior. Penny-pinchers tend to remain penny-pinchers, regardless of whether they accumulate a lot of money or not. Just look at Warren Buffett, who is renowned for his thrifty personal lifestyle.

If marketers aim to draw more 26-year-old HENRYs, with their significantly greater spending power now and in the future over middle-income consumers, they need to combine strategies borrowed from high-end brands, along with more mass-market tactics to send a clear message that these high-potential customers are understood, respected, and catered to.

Specifically, mass-marketing strategies must focus on value, so that the HENRYs get a greater return on their spending investment. This doesn't necessarily mean cheaper prices, but more value for the price asked.

This realization was eye-opening for JCPenney in its recent appliance offerings. The company assumed that its lower, value-priced refrigerators in the $899-$999 price range would be the strongest sellers. But millennials wanted the latest, greatest models with stainless steel or black finishes and more contemporary door styles. They were willing to pay up to $1,599 to $1,799 for the specific values they were looking for.

Meanwhile, luxury-focused strategies must be directed to delivering high-quality goods and services, including careful attention to superior materials and workmanship, and making customers feel pride of ownership for the items bought, as well as pride of belonging to the cadre of shoppers that are smart and in the know. This is the appeal of Shinola, hitting all the right notes in quality, style, workmanship and value, plus membership in a cool tribe of people that share the same values.

The recent *Wall Street Journal* article did an excellent job of identifying the customers within the 20-year millennial generational cohort that are pivotal for marketers to understand now in order to take them into the future.

But by ignoring their incomes and the spending potential that income affords, the article overlooked the single most vital data point in any marketer's strategic plan. The 26-year-old HENRYs, with incomes at the top 25 percent, are the bellwether consumers that will lead the cohort in spending and set the trends that the lower-income 26-year-olds will follow.

CASE STUDY: Shinola

Why Shinola Is a Brand HENRYs Love

The *New York Times* recently published a story about Shinola, famous for its 'Made in Detroit' watches, bicycles, and leather goods. It profiled how the company kick started a renaissance of growth and prosperity in Detroit.

Reporter Alex Williams wrote:

> As recently as a few years ago, when Mr. Kartsotis started his company [Shinola] known for its "Built in Detroit" watches, bicycles and leather goods, these blocks were on the fringe of an infamous skid row, the city was sliding toward bankruptcy, and the words "luxury" and "Detroit" were rarely paired outside the executive suites of Cadillac.
>
> Things are changing. The blocks surrounding Shinola's hangar-like retail outpost are now brimming with Brooklynesque designer housewares shops, selvage-jeans boutiques and farm-to-table restaurants, to the point that the upper Cass Corridor has become

"the luxury retail mecca of Midtown Detroit," as Curbed Detroit put it, "basically Shinola City."

Obviously Kartsotis and the Shinola brand have tapped into a new consumer market craving luxury in a brand new style. Not elitist or exclusionary luxury, but an expression of luxury that is relevant to the younger generation's eclectic and inclusive lifestyles. They want brands that are vibrant, individualistic and that reflect their core values.

That customer is a HENRY (high-earner-not-rich-yet). The HENRYs are young, highly-educated professionals, engineers, artisans, designers, managers, and entrepreneurs on the road to affluence.

Young HENRYs don't want their grandma's luxury brands, but their own – like Shinola.

Shinola is the face of new luxury

Perhaps there is no more contentious issue in the luxury market today than what makes a brand "real" luxury? The industry establishment frequently claims that this brand or that one simply doesn't measure up to their inbred standard, thus negating it as a competitive threat. But all that is changing, as the very definition of "luxury" is undergoing a paradigm shift in the consumer market.

In a recent survey conducted with over 600 luxury retailers and marketers by Unity Marketing and *Luxury Daily*, industry insiders identified the number-one threat disrupting the business of luxury as the change in customers' definition of luxury. Increasingly, luxury is becoming irrelevant with the result, as this insider said, "Luxury retailers and brands have lost their way."

Another insider expressed the quandary facing the luxury industry today: "The change in how consumers define luxury and the new path to purchase is dramatically redefining the marketing strategy. Luxury brands must be very agile and innovative in order to gain the favor of the new luxury consumer."

The luxury industry has an identity crisis. "The idea that luxury matters less and less to young people is a concern, as they will define what luxury means versus brands defining it via marketing efforts," said another.

HENRYs don't want their grandma's luxury brands, but their own — like Shinola.

The marketers' challenge is to translate their brand messages into values that are truly meaningful and relevant to today's customers' lifestyles and their increasingly sophisticated and informed mindset. But luxury marketers can't dictate anymore. They must follow the customers' lead, an idea foreign to the powers that be in the industry.

Many of the heritage luxury brands we know, like Louis Vuitton, Prada, Gucci, and Hermès, meet the 10 traditional values outlined below that define a luxury brand. But so too do many new-age brands, like Shinola. There are many in the luxury industry that would argue heatedly that Shinola may be many things, but it isn't a luxury brand. I'd argue just as strongly that it is indeed luxury, and I am confident many consumers would as well.

Let's examine each value more closely and how these values have been interpreted by Shinola in a way that makes the brand relevant to the HENRYs:

- **Superior performance** – A luxury brand connects with their customers by being at the top of its class, the best in its field. It must deliver better performance in some meaningful, measurable way.

Shinola's U.S.–built Runwell watch is the watch of presidents. President Bill Clinton has worn one for years and is said to have collected dozens of them. And President Obama is a huge fan, so much so that he commissioned the company to create a custom-made watch to gift to British Prime Minister David Cameron. It is as close as we come to the "British Royal Warrant" granted to tradespeople serving the Queen.

- **Craftsmanship** – Luxury brands connect with customers by presenting the highest quality and craftsmanship. The connection is intimate and personal, like the touch of the hand.

Shinola's Built-in-Detroit roots link to the craftsmanship and engineering embodied by the city as the country's automotive capital. In a watch factory located in a historic Detroit landmark building, once the home of GM's automotive research lab, the company hand-assembles every Shinola watch.

- **Exclusivity** – Luxury brands connect with customers by making them feel special and unique through the presentation of a special, unique experience. Exclusivity today is less about excluding people from enjoying the brand or limiting access; rather, it is about making customers and brand loyalists feel a member of an exclusive community linked by shared values and ideals.

Adweek proclaimed Shinola "the coolest brand in the world." Who wouldn't want to belong to that tribe? And its story of revitalizing American manufacturing resonates deeply with the zeitgeist of today's consumer culture.

- **Innovation** – Luxury brands connect with customers by presenting new visions and new ideas, all in keeping with the core values of the brand.

Shinola's entire brand myth is based on the idea of innovation, rebirth, and creative ingenuity. It is reflected in its products and processes, as well as in its design of retail locations. With built-in-Detroit its core value, the company recently paid tribute to the city's musical roots by creating a line of audiophile equipment of turntables, headphones, and speakers.

- **Sense of Place and Time** – Luxury brands connect by being both timely, grounded in the here and now, and timeless, transcending time from the past to the future.

Shinola's 'Built in Detroit' tagline says it all. It hearkens back to the past century's industrial revolution and looks forward to the future with 21st-century engineering and manufacturing prowess. But its sense of place and time extends to its retail outlets, each individually designed to be grounded in its local community, like its new Brooklyn flagship store housed on the DUMBO waterfront in a former coffee warehouse.

- **Sophistication and Design Aesthetic** – Luxury brands connect with an appreciation of the customers' sophistication celebrated through the brand's unique design aesthetic.

From its watches to its bicycles, leather goods, writing journals and other products, Shinola prides itself on a distinctive and unique design aesthetic that is both classic and contemporary. Its flagship stores also showcase the brand's unique vision, which its creative director Daniel Caudill describes as the "intersection of clean minimalism and 1930s industrialism."

- **Creative Expression** – Luxury brands connect through the spark of artistic creativity as interpreted through the eyes of a designer or visionary.

Shinola calls out the creativity of its "makers" in an online journal that features stories about its designers. Shinola's makers celebrate the hard work and creative expression of the everyday journeyman, masters of their trade and craft, much like Messrs. Vuitton, Prada, Gucci and Hermès did in their day.

- **Relevant** – Luxury brands connect by being relevant to their customers' lives and lifestyle. Relevancy makes the brand special and bespoke for the individual.

With aims to become a true lifestyle brand, Shinola continues to tap its creative team and manufacturing expertise in creating new and unexpected products across a whole range of lifestyle endeavors. Besides its core watch, bicycle and leather goods offerings, the company has dog leashes and other pet accessories, footballs and sporting goods, pocket knives and screw driver sets, apparel, travel guides, and latest on deck, a line of Shinola jewelry.

- **Heritage** – Luxury brands connect with their customer through the story of its lineage and provenance.

Though it was only founded in 2011, Shinola takes its name from a 1907 shoe polish company that became part of the American cultural myth when a disgruntled World War II soldier polished his commander's boots with poop, proclaiming that he "wouldn't know shit from Shinola." Late-night show host Jimmy Kimmel refreshed his older viewer's memories, or introduced it for the first time to others, in a mock game show skit "Can You Tell S#*t from Shinola?".

- **Responsibility** – Luxury brands connect with their customers on a platform of social responsibility and giving back and doing good.

Shinola's interpretation of corporate responsibility is nothing less than bringing manufacturing jobs and investment dollars back to Detroit. Many of its philanthropic endeavors are focused on rebuilding Detroit, with a recent project creating a dog park and green alleys near its company headquarters. And in partnership with the FEED Project, it designed a line of canvas and leather FEED bags, with the proceeds donated to Detroit's only food rescue organization, Forgotten Harvest.

The Title of a "Luxury Brand" Must Be Earned

The title of "luxury brand" must be earned. A brand can't claim the label for itself. While brands that aspire to the designation of luxury share these 10 core values, each brand must interpret and express its luxury distinctly and in such a way that is authentic unto itself and that resonates in the minds of its customers.

Whether a heritage luxury, like Louis Vuitton, Prada, Gucci and Hermès, or new luxury, like Shinola, the real luxury of the brand isn't only or mostly about its products, its manufacturing processes, its design and style or its service. It's about a commitment to each of these values, from those working on the shop floor to the corner office and into the store where it connects with customers.

Luxury isn't a product or a price point, but a mindset. The core values expressed by the brand must link the company and its staff's dedication to quality with the customers' values and aspirations. It's these people, not the product, that make a luxury brand.

Or as another luxury insider said, "The name of the luxury game needs to change. It's not about the brands, it's about the people and how you make them feel – status over others is so passé!"

Luxury isn't a product or a price point, but a mindset.

CASE STUDY: Gucci

How Gucci reinvented a heritage luxury brand for a new generation

Kering, the global luxury group with brands including **Bottega Veneta**, **Saint Laurent**, **Balenciaga**, **Brioni**, and others, has been going gangbusters, with sales up 25 percent from 2016 to 2017.

Leading Kering's charge in year-over-year growth is **Gucci**, its Italian luxury fashion and leather goods brand. Gucci's revenues were up 42 percent over 2016. Gucci alone makes up 57 percent of its Luxury Activities segment, which accounts for 71 percent of total corporate revenues of $15.5 billion in 2017. Stunning results in a luxury market that Bain & Company reports grew 5 percent in 2017.

Even more impressive, Kering's chairman and CEO Francois-Henri Pinault told CNBC that about 50 percent of Gucci's sales are coming from millennials, the cohort of 35-year-olds and younger, a generation that has been particularly troubling for luxury brands.

"It means that we have a core category of customers that are between 25 and 35 . . . The attractiveness of couture, of ready-to-wear is much higher for that clientele than it used to be for older people," he said. While Pinault doesn't identify the income levels of these millennial customers, their age range suggests that young HENRYs are well represented among its customers.

In capturing the attention and dollars of millennials, numerous analysts attribute Gucci's success to its industry-leading internet strategies and how the company has managed to integrate digital connection and the in-store experience to present a true omnichannel, or channel-agnostic, customer experience.

Gucci's achievements in the digital space, millennials' native channel, are remarkable. L2 Research, which specializes in data-driven analysis, gave its top spot for best performing digital fashion brand to Gucci in 2016 and it hung onto that position in 2017. L2's measure of a fashion brand's "digital competence" includes website and e-commerce, digital marketing, social media and mobile. In those key measures it outranks Michael Kors, Fendi, Burberry, and Louis Vuitton, its closest digital-savvy brands.

But rather than attribute Gucci's success to its industry-leading digital performance, it is rather a sign or marker of the brand's success, like its financial reports. Gucci's phenomenal performance, especially among millennials, is not caused by its digital competence, as good as it is. Rather its success is directly attributed to the dream team that is spearheading the brand's resurgence – CEO Marco Bizzarri and creative director Alessandro Michele.

Gucci's dream team

Bizzarri took over the mantle at Gucci in December 2014, replacing Patrizio di Marco who led the company from 2009. Di Marco's exit prompted then creative director Frida Giannini to leave as well. This left Bizzarri with his first big executive decision.

Intuition and instinct are more important than rationality.

Michele was an unlikely choice for creative director, though he had joined the company in 2002 under Tom Ford and worked as associate designer to Giannini from 2011. Bizzarri says Michele wasn't on his list of creative director candidates, but a chance meeting of the two sealed the deal when Bizzarri went in search of someone in the company who could school him on the process of design.

"Intuition and instinct are more important than rationality," Bizzarri said at a 2017 WWD Summit to explain his gut choice of Michele as Gucci's next creative director. The two were completely sympatico. "We were thinking the same way – for me, it was from a business standpoint, and for him, design. It was very much about empathy. You feel like you found the right person immediately."

Early on they established clear divisions of labor and responsibilities, Bizzarri for business and Michele in creative design. It is said that Bizzarri doesn't discuss sales or budgets with Michele, and gives him free rein to express his creativity with no boundaries. "You cannot put limits or constraints on creativity," Bizzarri said. To that end, he has put creativity at the center of Gucci as a brand and backed it up with corporate values that foster creativity, including "respect, happiness, passion, empowerment and inclusivity."

Redesigning Gucci for the next generation

To reinvent Gucci, the Bizzarri-Michele dream team knew they had to get rid of outmoded ideas that were holding the brand back. So out went the corporate office black-and-white pictures of past celebrities that were historically the face of the brand, like Grace Kelly and Jacqueline Kennedy Onassis. Instead Gucci now dresses contemporary style icons that resonate with millennials, like Rhianna, Blake Lively, Brad Pitt, Rachel McAdams and Selma Hayek, not surprising as she is wife of Kering CEO Pinault. Sir Elton John is a friend of Michele's and was the inspiration for many fashions shown at Gucci's spring/summer 2018 show.

And while the previous di Marco-Giannini team de-emphasized the Gucci GG logo in design, Bizzarri and

Michele dug into the company archives and resurrected its GG logo to feature it prominently on handbags and other accessories, as well as bringing forward the Dionysus buckle for some shoes and handbags. The results were immediate. Six out of seven of Gucci's best-selling and high-margin accessories have been created by Michele, Bizzarri told the Julius Baer Global Advisory Board this year.

But Michele has been given room to play with the classic GG logo, a freedom hard to imagine at any other luxury brand. In an unprecedented move, Michele invited graffiti artist Trevor Andrew, aka GucciGhost, to collaborate in Gucci's fall collection for 80 pieces. Where other luxury brands would more likely file a lawsuit against such logo tampering, Michele embraced it, which says volumes about how Bizzarri and Michele look at the world and Gucci's evolving role in it.

Anticipating more demand for the new Gucci image, the company is adding a 35,000 square foot manufacturing facility in Italy, called the Gucci Art Lab to produce leather goods and shoes. The goal is to be more responsive to growing consumer demand, as well as to enhance capabilities for the company to source and manufacture in a sustainable fashion, including its recent ban on the use of fur in its products.

Business developments

On the business side as well, Gucci boutiques are getting a makeover. So far 25 percent of its 550 stores have been remodeled under its "New Store Concept," intended to marry the in-store shopping experience with its digital platform. By the end of the year 30 more stores will be overhauled, according to Kering CFO Jean-Marc Duplaix.

With the creative energy of Michele and Bizzarri's business acumen, plus his hands-off management approach on the creative side, this dream team is ready for whatever comes next for the Gucci brand. But we can be assured that whatever it is, it will be new and different and aimed squarely at the next-generation customers that are the future of the Gucci brand.

"Millennials tend to have an appetite for new things and they are driven by content, emotions and personal connections. They value self-expression and they value sustainability," as Bizzarri told the Julius Baer group.

Who Are the HENRYs?

Why Every Brand Needs to Understand Them

Today many brands and retailers are stuck in a slow-growth or worse no-growth mode, desperate to find new opportunities and new customers with both an appetite for their goods and services and a budget to afford them. They need to meet the HENRYs – an emerging consumer segment that holds the key to the American consumer economy's future.

The HENRYs are the mass affluent who think of themselves as "middle class," but with household incomes $100k–$249.9k, they are doing better than 75 percent of all U.S. households. Yet they remain below the Ultra-affluent income levels of the top three-to-five percent, on which luxury brands traditionally focus.

For marketers from mass to "class," households at the top income range ($100k+) are critically important, as their numbers are growing fast.

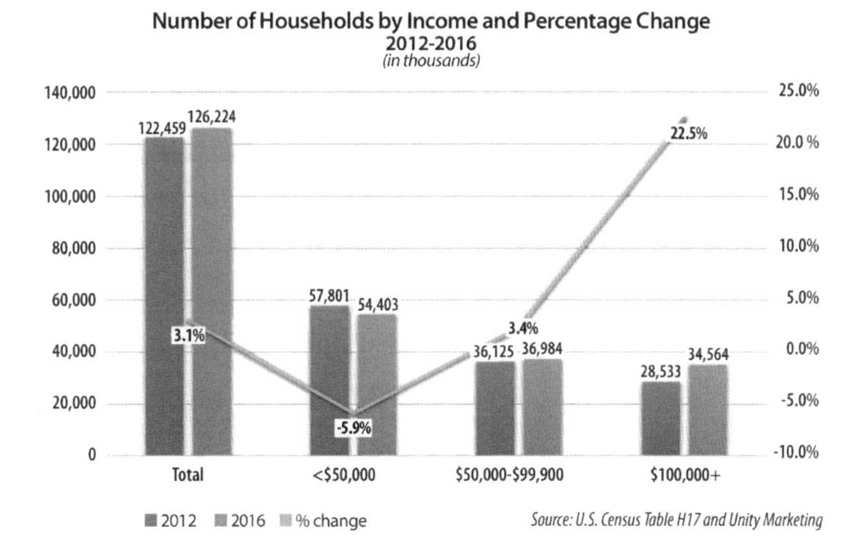

From 2012 to 2016 the number of U.S. households grew by a mere 3.1 percent, from 122.4 to 126.2 million, but most of that growth has been in the higher-income $100,000-and-over segment, according to the latest census.

The sad reality of the current consumer economy is that the American middle class has lost much of its spending power, leaving brands that have traditionally targeted this customer – think **Macy's**, **JCPenney**, **Gap**, **Target**, **Kohl's** – to search out new consumer segments that offer better growth possibilities.

If the middle-income customer is scarce, the logical place for marketers to look for growth is one step up the income ladder: the HENRYs.

That is exactly what **Walmart**, the world's largest retailer, is in the process of doing.

CASE STUDY: Walmart

Walmart's mass-to-class strategy

Walmart is undergoing a massive corporate makeover. With $500.3 billion in total revenues worldwide in fiscal 2018, 11,700 stores and 2.3 million associates, it is a long-term project that will take place on many fronts. Change and corporate transformation in its business and culture were CEO Doug McMillon's primary theme in remarks at the June 1, 2018 Walmart Associate and Shareholders Meeting.

With the U.S. Walmart segment accounting for 64 percent of total sales, or $318.5 billion alone, including nearly 5,000 stores and its e-commerce business, the U.S. is where the stakes are highest and where its eventual transformation will be measured.

At the 2018 National Retail Federation Big Show, where McMillon was honored as The Visionary at the NRF Foundation Gala, he told the story of the company's awakening to the need for change. "At some point, Walmart became big and societal expectations changed. And we missed the memo."

It wasn't just societal changes that Walmart missed, but demographic shifts as well. Its core customer base of lower-to-middle income consumers are losing ground to higher-income consumers with greater spending power and much higher expectations of what they want when doing business with a company like Walmart.

Driven by necessity

Walmart's average customer has an income of only $56,482, according to Kanter Retail, so its core customer base is shrinking. It simply has no choice but to figure out ways to entice the more affluent customers whose income has outgrown Walmart's basic marketing message of "Everyday Low Prices (EDLP)." By necessity it has to align with affluent consumers.

In describing the new Walmart, McMillon continually refers to it as a "technology company." In its first moves upmarket, tech has been its primary vehicle.

It got a jumpstart in expanding its e-commerce platform with the acquisition of **Jet.com** in 2016 which brought over tech-entrepreneur Marc Lore to head up Walmart's digital division. Then it acquired **hayneedle.com, shoes.com, moosejaw.com, modcloth.com, bonobos.com**, and the new bedding site **allswell.com**. Combined with jet.com and walmart.com, e-commerce accounts for $11.8 billion in sales, a mere drop in the bucket.

Just added to Walmart's e-commerce platform is a new premium brand shop under partnership with **Lord & Taylor**. This greatly expands Walmart's brand width to include 125 luxury-leaning fashion brands.

Denise Incandela heads up Walmart's digital fashion group and she comes with impressive luxury-fashion credentials after serving as president global digital at Ralph Lauren and EVP and CMO at Saks Fifth Avenue.

Selections on the walmart.com premium brands shop are in keeping with Walmart's more affordable prices and far less extensive than found on the lordandtaylor.com site. However, it is an interesting partnership, but whether it will move the needle for either company is a question.

Time saved is money earned

For the HENRY shopper, time is money and Walmart has been working overtime to make shopping time efficient.

> **For the HENRY shopper, time is money.**

Two-day delivery, curbside pickup and more self-check-out stations are designed to give customers fast, efficient access to its product range and cost savings. A new home installation and assembly for furniture and entertainment systems through the Handy home-services provider also makes these expensive purchases more appealing to the time-starved affluents.

To further serve the personal service needs of the affluent, Walmart just announced a new JetBlack service, the brainchild of Rent the Runway's cofounder Jenny Fleiss. In her role at Walmart she heads up the company's Store N°8 technology incubator, whose mission is to "Create the future of retail."

Jetblack is Store N°8's first launch, now in test-mode in New York City. It is described as a personal shopping service that, "uses a combination of artificial intelligence practices and expertise from professional buyers across the home, health, parenting, fashion and wellness categories, as well as parents themselves. Some everyday essentials may be sourced from Walmart and Jet.com, while other items and specialty products are procured from local brands and shops." Orders can be placed by text message with delivery promised same day. How the AI works, I am not exactly sure.

As a membership service, it carries a premium price tag of $600 per year. It has some of my fellow members on the Forbes.com contributor team scratching their heads. Neil Stern questions whether the $50-a-month price tag will deliver real value to customers, who may be jaded by the affiliation with the parent company. But he applauds the company for thinking outside the box.

Paula Rosenblum said on LinkedIn, "I'd rather hire a human personal shopper and get it done in a month, but I don't need AI to remind me I need paper towels. Maybe the logic and market will become clear to me one day, but not yet."

New corporate consciousness

In recognizing that retail is now a people-first business much of McMillon's focus for the company is to rehabilitate its tarnished reputation as a corporate citizen and an employer. To this end, the company has been very proactive, raising hourly wages, expanding maternity benefits and it just announced a program to subsidize the cost of a two- and four-year degree program in

Business and Supply Chain Management through partnership with Guild Education and three universities.

By taking better care of its employees, the company hopes they will take better care of the 270 million customers served each week. And by supporting its workers, it is also supporting the many communities where those workers live. At the shareholders meeting, McMillon explained how Walmart is working to strengthen the local communities it serves, through support of neighborhoods affected by natural disasters, sustainable sourcing of products, and deploying renewable energy.

Retail is now a people-first business.

"The people we serve in communities not only trust us to be there when disaster strikes. They also want to feel good about our social and environmental impact and trust the products we sell are good for their kids and the planet," he stated.

By raising the corporate consciousness of Walmart, it will position the company in line with the values of the affluent who demand such high standards from the companies they do business with.

A new upwardly-mobile Walmart for HENRYs?

Walmart has very publicly committed itself to change. "Meaningful change is rarely easy but it's essential for success in the future," McMillon said at the shareholders meeting. Part of that change has to be to cultivate a more affluent customer, one who isn't going to be easy to attract to its local Supercenter stores, which account for 75 percent of its U.S. storefronts.

Looking from the outside in, I see Walmart's current efforts to appeal to higher-income customers as baby steps in a bigger strategy down the road. The company's basic DNA still is "Everyday Low Prices," not everyday great value or everyday great service or everyday great quality, which is what affluent consumers are looking for.

To succeed in marketing to the affluent, the culture built on EDLP has to change. But there still are plenty of people that Walmart serves that need the low prices that it offers. It will be a very challenging tightrope for the company to walk.

At the same time, Walmart has the resources in place to make crossing the divide from mass to class possible in its dream team of retail tech visionaries – and all experts marketing to HENRYs – Marc Lore, Denise Incandela, Jenny Fleiss, and Andy Dunn (bonobos.com). They have been in their roles at Walmart for only a short time, barely long enough to begin to figure out the complexities of a corporate structure the size of Walmart.

If they stay around long enough to chart the waters, and don't bail too soon as ModCloth CEO Matt Kaness did after only one year, Walmart is in a good position to turn its upmarket dreams into a reality. But it may not be enough to do it all online. It will have to open real doors to welcome the affluent shoppers, and it won't be the Walmart Supercenter off the highway.

Why HENRYs Matter

Consumers remain extremely cautious about spending with good reason, as the average U.S. household's income is only about 4.3 percent more now ($83,143) than it was at the turn of the century ($79,649 in 2016 dollars), according to the latest Census reports.

But while household average income has gone up, the underlying structure on which household income is calculated has changed dramatically since the start of the century. In 2000 those at the top 5 percent of U.S, households had an income starting at $145,220 and an average income of $252,400 (in 2016 dollars).

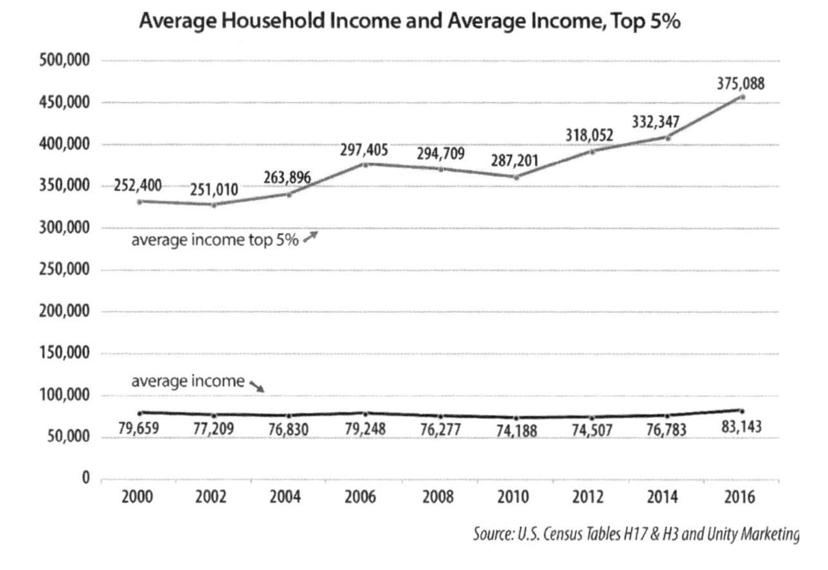

Source: U.S. Census Tables H17 & H3 and Unity Marketing

Today the top 5 percent of U.S. households are defined as those with incomes of $225,251 or more, according to Census table h1. That is a 55 percent increase in the income required to rank in the top 5 percent.

Their average income rose 48.6 percent from 2000 to 2016, by contrast the U.S. average household income only rose 4.3 percent. What that really means is the incomes among the highest-earners have grown far faster than those in the middle-and-lower income segments.

The rich have indeed gotten richer in the 21st century. And while the HENRYs, household income from $100k–$249.9k, are not rich yet, they are indeed much richer than the typical American household.

HENRYs are 'heavy-lifters' in the consumer economy

There are about 30 million American HENRY households, nearly 25 percent of the nation's 126 million households. They sit below the 5 million Ultra-affluent households by income ($250k and above), but above the 96 million middle-and-lower-income households.

Within the HENRY income segment those at the lower-end of the income scale, with incomes $100k–$124.9k, are the most prevalent, making up nearly 40 percent of the HENRY total.

Whether these lower-income HENRYs are called upper-middle income or lower-income affluent, they along with the remaining 19 million HENRY households account for nearly 40 percent of total U.S. consumer expenditures. The Ultra-affluents with their significantly greater spending power, though far fewer numbers, make up only about 10 to 15 percent of total consumer spending.

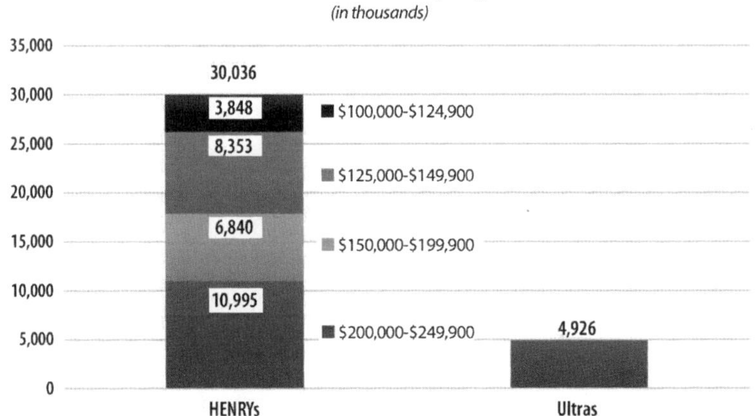

Source: U.S. Census Table HINC06 and Unity Marketin

That means the spending power of an affluent household is twice as big as the average middle-class one. They are the "heavy lifting" customer across the entire retailing landscape.

Of course, all affluent households aren't created equal in spending power, with the Ultra-affluents, who correspond to the top 3 percent of households by income (or roughly 4.9 million households with incomes starting at about $250,000), endowed with much more discretionary income and wealth.

The problem is that the high-spending Ultra-affluent consumers are thin on the ground. There are six HENRY households for every Ultra-affluent one. HENRYs are the mass-affluent and far more plentiful in numbers.

With the traditional middle-class market shrinking, HENRYs are a growing, dynamic customer segment with discretion to spend. HENRYs, especially the younger

HENRYs, are the new target customer for mass-market brands and the future for luxury brands, as most people start on the road to affluence as HENRYs.

But it's going to take more years before the highest earning members of the young HENRY segment start to reach Ultra-affluent levels of income. So between now and the middle of the next decade, HENRYs will offer the best growth prospects for brands and retailers, high-end, low-end, or in the middle.

HENRYs Get No Respect in Luxury Circles

For luxury brands that aim at the wealthiest and most affluent consumers, i.e., the Ultras, the lower-income, mass-affluent HENRYs are an often overlooked group that, quoting Rodney Dangerfield, "gets no respect." Yet these are the next-generation customers that luxury brands must cultivate for their future.

Looking across the 35 million affluent income segment, HENRYs comprise 85 percent of the affluent consumer market. And while many luxury marketers battle fiercely for the Ultra-affluent market, they neglect the HENRYs. This is a huge missed opportunity.

Young HENRYs are the 'heaviest lifters' among the heavy lifters

The HENRYs term was originally coined by Shawn Tully in a *Fortune* magazine article in 2003 focused on the segment's heavy tax burden. I have, however, applied it to the income demographics defining those between the mass-middle and luxury upper-income class.

While HENRYs are distributed across all age ranges, the young HENRYs, aged 24 to 44, are significantly more important for most marketers not aimed specifically at providing goods and services for the mature consumer segment.

Incomes rise with age, peaking from age 35 to 54, after which people start to retire, which tends to drive down the overall income of those aged 55 to 64. So for both HENRYs and Ultra-affluents the ages of 45 to 54 specifically are when both segments' peak in terms of size and spending power.

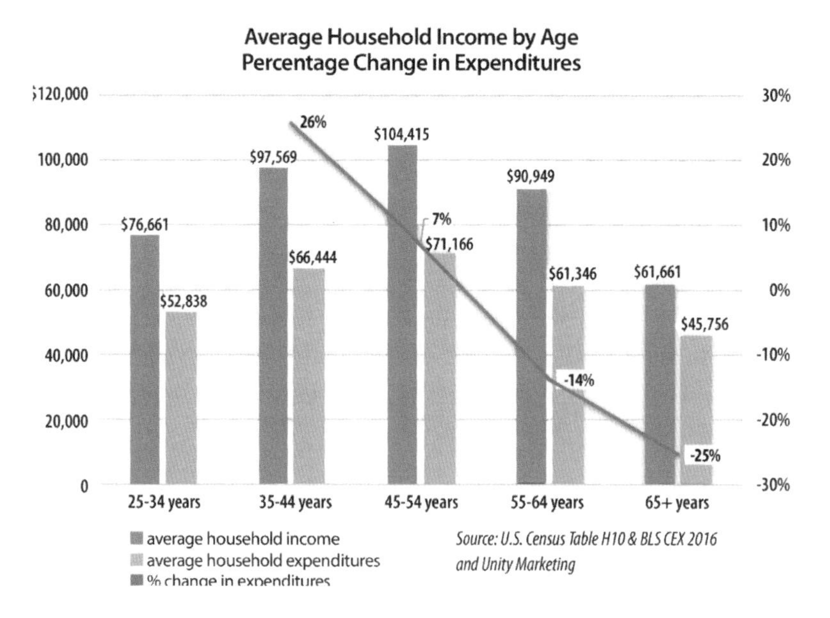

But the biggest increase in household spending occurs when the head of household is aged 35 to 44, rising 26 percent overall from expenditures by those aged 25–34

years. By contrast, when consumers reach the next age range, 45–54 years, their expenditures rise only 7 percent, and fall steadily thereafter.

However, HENRYs are far more heavily represented in the younger age ranges, 25–34 years than Ultra-affluents, as the younger HENRYs are developing in their careers with many of the most ambitious on the road to the Ultra levels of affluence.

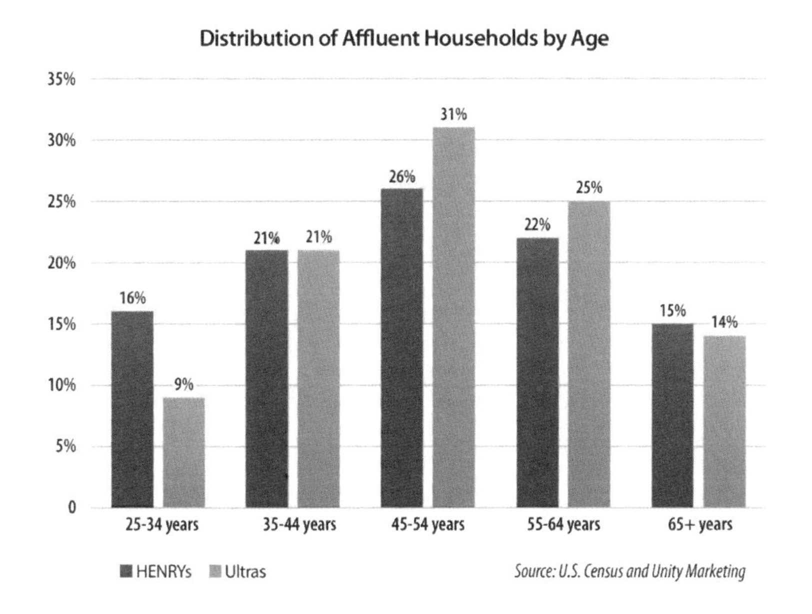

Consumers' spending makes predictable shifts as people age

For years financial expert and author Harry Dent, who studies business and consumer demographic cycles, has warned about shifts in consumer spending caused by the aging of the baby boomers, the largest generation in history.

Boomers are now retreating in the generation's predictable lifecycle spending wave, and the millennials, the next big generational wave, is only beginning to start its climb.

"The baby boom generation peaked in their spending cycle in 2007," Dent explains, noting that between ages 46 and 51, consumer spending achieves its lifelong high, but declines rapidly after that.

"The largest generation in history will spend less money as they age," Dent says. "They spend most of their money raising kids and when the kids leave the nest, they don't have to buy so much stuff in malls and at retail."

"The next big generation of millennials will be spending more money as they age, but they haven't even fully entered the work force yet and about half of the millennials are still in school," Dent continues. "Until the millennials get large enough to start driving the economy back up again, which we predict will start in about 2023, the boomers will have a downward impact on the economy." This downward trend, Dent notes, takes into account the impact of immigration.

Millennials, aged 18–38, are vital to every brands' future, as they are "entering prime spending years as they buy homes and make improvements. Their outlays are growing as more of the generation moves into adulthood." Further the millennials with high educational attainment and professional careers will take the lead early in income against their peers and their spread will continue to grow as they mature.

Thus the HENRY millennials' importance to marketers will only continue to grow until about age 50 when their household spending will peak, 12 to 32 years from now, according to Dent's spending wave research.

➲ OPPORTUNITY: Home Furnishings

Young HENRYs Are Primed for Home-Related Products and Services

Assessing the marketing opportunity with HENRYs requires understanding their shopping and purchase behaviors. Past purchase behavior is typically a good predictor of future purchasing behavior, as consumers are more or less creatures of habit and so they tend to follow similar paths to purchase that worked successfully for them in the past.

Typical Purchase Behavior

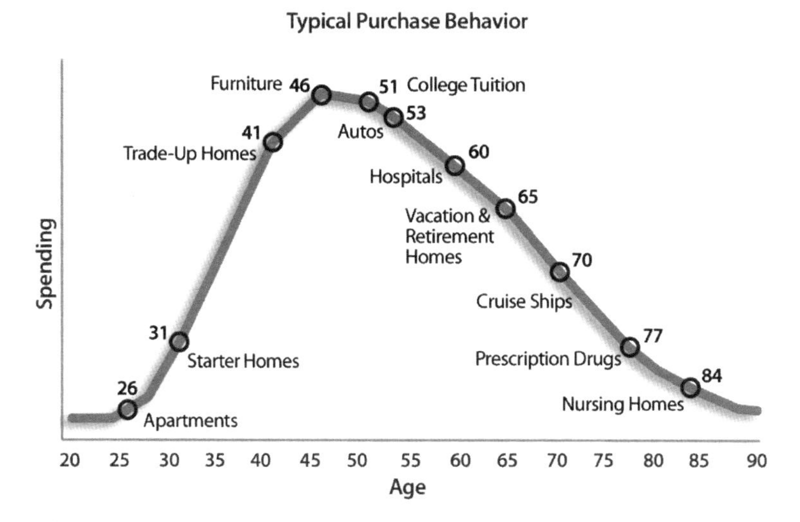

Source: U.S. Census Bureau, Dent Research

The Bureau of Labor Statistics Consumer Expenditure survey, the nation's authority on consumer spending and the source used by policy makers in the federal government, identifies two key consumer segments where expenditures on household furnishings and equipment peak: People aged 35–44 and those with household incomes over $100,000.

Admittedly, spending on home furnishings continues to be strong for those aged 45–64 years and rises as income rises over $100,000, but since almost all of tomorrow's Ultra-affluents start out as young HENRYs, these are the best customers for home marketers to make a connection with today that can lead to growth and prosperity tomorrow.

Connecting with the younger HENRYs is even more vital for home marketers' strategy because as they mature, HENRYs' housing needs are likely to change. From ages 25 to 34, young people are in the household formation stage, starting their families, and often buying their first homes. From ages 35 to 44, they are likely to move up to their second homes and continue adding to their families.

In the mature life stages, from 45–64 years, consumer salso make predictable changes in their homes as they perhaps move up again, or invest in a second home. Then as children leave the nest and retirement approaches, they may move again to a smaller home, all the while continuing to have the need for new home furnishings and home decorating solutions.

CASE STUDY: Ikea

Ikea understands young HENRYs

The recent passing of Ikea founder Ingvar Kamprad has revived attention to a retailer that is frequently overlooked in home furnishings circles. All too often it is the butt of jokes. From the unintelligible instructions required to assemble its furniture and the unpronounceable names for the 9,500 products it sells, to its meatballs, Ikea is more often laughed at than taken seriously by people in the home business.

"The home furnishings industry across the board doesn't have Ikea on their radar," says Warren Shoulberg, former editorial director for several Progressive Business Media home furnishings business publications. "When home furnishings retailers talk about their competition, I never hear anybody talk about Ikea. That is going to be a huge mistake."

Ikea ranks

In reality, Ikea is a powerhouse of innovative home furnishing ideas and experiential retailing that places it second to none in furnishing American's homes, from the kitchen cabinets, including all the stuff in the drawers and cabinets, to the bedroom, bathroom, living room, and dining room.

While Ikea generates just about half the sales of top-ranked U.S. home retailer **Bed Bath & Beyond** – $6.1 billion, to $12.2 billion – it does so out of fewer than

50 stores, as compared with over 1,500 for Bed Bath & Beyond, and with a much broader product range. With that, Ikea is the second-largest home retailer in the country today.

While Ikea may be given short shrift among those in the home furnishings industry, it ranks among many others. It's No. 41 overall on the *Forbes* list of the world's most valuable brands. And among retailers on that list, it is behind only Walmart (No. 24), **Home Depot** (No. 34) and **H&M** (No. 36).

Consumers also know Ikea and value it. The Reputation Institute places Ikea No. 58 among the world's most reputable brands in its 2017 Global RepTrak 100 listing. And the more familiar people are with Ikea, the stronger its reputation. Further, among the consumers who count the most and will propel Ikea into the future – millennials – Ikea's reputation is strongest.

Ikea is ramping up in the U.S.

Ikea is on the move, and soon home furnishings retailers won't have the luxury of ignoring it any longer. Despite its furniture-in-a-box model, it lagged in e-commerce strategies but that is changing.

Initially choosing to drive customers to its stores via its website, Ikea has made online e-commerce a priority. Now customers can buy online and pick up orders in 31 of its 47 U.S. stores. It has also implemented lower shipping costs for customers in the Northeast, to follow with the same across the country.

After opening four new stores in 2017, Ikea plans to

add three more in 2018 and another three in 2019 and is building two additional customer fulfillment centers in the States.

Regarding its plans, Lars Petersson, president of Ikea U.S., told *USA Today,* "In the U.S., we are committed to expanding our shopping experience with new retail locations, enhanced technology and greater accessibility for customers."

Home furnishings retailers won't have the luxury of ignoring Ikea any longer.

"Ikea is being much more aggressive," says Shoulberg. "People are remembering back in the day when they didn't have American-sized bedding or when their styles weren't matched to American tastes. But you go into Ikea now, and their design aesthetic is much more attuned to North America, everything is in the right sizes, and they are doing a big kitchen business. I continue to be impressed by what they are doing."

Shoulberg identified seven pillars of Ikea's prominence in the home furnishings market in an article for *The Robin Report*, "Is Ikea the most influential retailer of the past 25 years?" Here's an overview.

Merchandising: Solutions for every home need today, forget about tomorrow

The traditional furniture retail model is based on the idea of investing in pieces that will last a lifetime. But that is totally foreign to many Americans, who the Census Department estimates will move on average 11 times in their lifetime. Ikea's buy it now, use it now, and forget about tomorrow is perfectly in sync with millennials' mindset.

"Ikea was like Xanax for home furnishings, instantly relieving the stress and anxiety of making a big-ticket purchase," Shoulberg writes in his article. "It's a seminal change in the home business and one that conventional furniture stores are still trying to come to grips with, for the most part unsuccessfully."

Products: Clean, basic and scaled right

Back in 1985 when Ikea first landed on America's shores, its modern Scandinavian style and smaller scale were largely foreign to American tastes. But since then Americans have grown into favoring its clean, basic, simplistic lines. "This is exactly the design aesthetic that every store in America is going after today and Ikea has been there for decades," Shoulberg writes. "They have Gen Y written all over them."

Pricing: Ultimate affordability

Ikea has created a pricing perception of being inexpensive without being cheap. "They are insanely inexpensive when compared to similar products at stores like **West Elm**, **CB2** or even **Bed Bath & Beyond**," he notes, adding that people don't feel like they are buying "cheap crap" when shopping at Ikea.

Stores: True shopping destinations

Going to an Ikea store is a true shopping experience, from the Swedish meatballs to the maze-like path customers are led through where they experience all that the store offers, like it or not.

Ikea stores are designed to get people to spend hours inside, which makes them true destinations. "Its locations remain places where people go on purpose with the intent of buying," Shoulberg explains. "There are great display vignettes, lots of selling-floor excitement and all kinds of multiple assortments so that even if you miss it the first time, you'll see it three or four more times before you're done."

Marketing: Catalogs are still dream books

Since the beginning, Ikea's annual catalog has been the hallmark of its marketing efforts. Not a catalog marketer per se, Ikea's catalog is a dream book to imagine what an Ikea-furnished life would be like. More than a directory of products, Shoulberg wrote it is "page after page of romance, giving shoppers decorating ideas, design direction and lifestyle imaging."

Ikea is also stepping up its marketing through more television spots and print, with advertising that is relevant to the cultural issues of our time, for example featuring gay and bi-racial couples.

In a new ad, Ikea asks "Where did the American dream go?" with messages that "Today, it's not about having more, but being more," and "Today, it's not about 'bigger is better,' but about having smaller, more meaningful experiences."

Sourcing: Private labels, exclusive designs

Every one of the 9,500 products it sells and the 2,500 new products introduced each year, Ikea designs and sources directly. While it doesn't own all its manufacturing, it buys no products off the shelf.

Being so vertically integrated, Ikea can deliver on its promise of being "planet positive" and transition to a "circular economy," as it states in its 2017 yearly group summary. So it invests in recycled and environmentally sound and responsibly sourced materials and is committed to being a responsible company across all sectors it works in and all constituencies it serves, including its employees.

Name: Unforgettable

And Shoulberg concludes his assessment of Ikea's pillars for growth with its distinctive and unforgettable name. Its name is a mashup of founder Ingvar Kamprad initials, the farm where he grew up, Elmtaryd, and his hometown of Agunnaryd. And not only is the company's name memorable but so are its product names, said to originate with Kamprad being dyslexic so he needed names he could remember to classify products, even if we can't pronounce them.

In the United States today there are just over 100 major

metropolitan statistical areas with over half-a-million people. By year's end, Ikea will have half of them covered. It's time for Ikea to become recognized by the home furnishings community as the powerhouse competitor it is. Forewarned is forearmed.

Young HENRYs' Dream Home

Not only are young HENRYs decorating their homes differently, they are also choosing to live in different kinds of homes than previous generations. They aren't necessarily buying the old mantra that "bigger is better" when it comes to home, nor that they should buy the most expensive homes that their income can allow. They have a new idea of the American Dream Home and are living it.

HENRYs' values shift

Back in 2008 John Zogby, founder of the Zogby International Poll, predicted a seismic shift in American's aspirations, values and ideals in his book *The Way We'll Be: The Zogby Report on the Transformation of the American Dream.*

Zogby identified four mega-trends that are shaping the trajectory of the American culture and fundamentally redefining the American Dream and the homes that have come to embody that dream. They are:

- **Living with limits:** Leaner, smaller, more personal and personalized

- **Embracing diversity:** Global, networked and inclusive
- **Looking inward**: Who I am, not what I own
- **Demanding authenticity:** Searching for authenticity in a make-believe world

He wrote:

> "Our polling consistently shows not only that wealth isn't being shared equally – that's obvious – but that average Americans have made fundamental adjustments in their expectations, their needs and their values, and that those adjustments are creating whole new paradigms through which people are making consumption and political choices that will shape the nation in the decades to come."

The American culture is at a crossroads, after more than half a century of material-driven consumption that defined the American Dream as getting more and more stuff to fill bigger and bigger houses.

Coinciding with the Great Recession, although the seeds of this paradigm shift were forming at least since the turn of the century, Americans started to wake up to the realization that their extravagant buying and spending ways were not making them any happier or personally fulfilled. Quite the opposite. The tide started to turn from a drive focused on quantity of things to quality of life, since the one clearly wasn't leading to the other.

American dream homes

Fast-forward to today, and Zogby is out with a new book, *We Are Many, We Are One: Neo-Tribes and Tribal Analytics in 21st Century America*, and a new poll that shows just how far the pendulum has swung in the consciousness of American consumers and the home that is their American Dream.

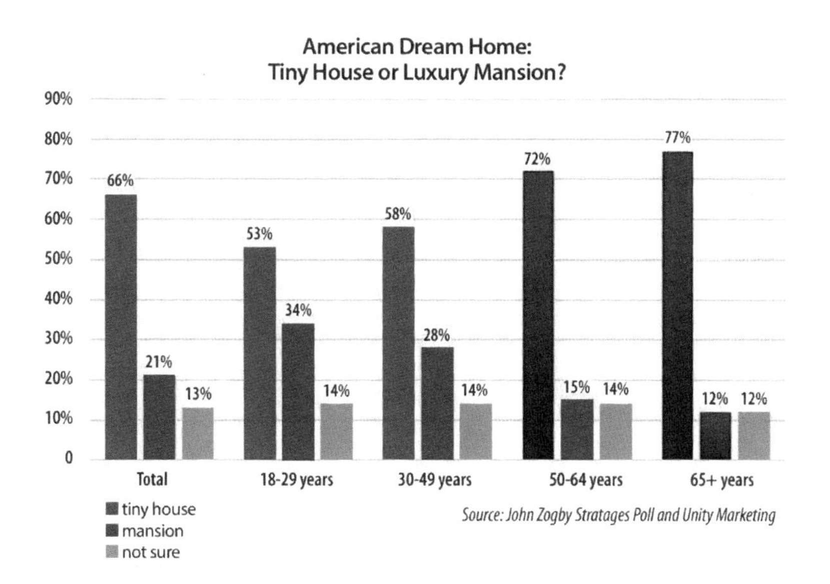

Zogby polled n=800 American consumers and asked them to imagine two romanticized styles of living:

- A grand mansion with lots of amenities, located in an expensive and prestigious neighborhood
- A well-constructed tiny home, off the grid, surrounded by beautiful and bountiful nature

The overall results didn't surprise me with the back-to-nature home the winner, but the wide difference in distribution of the responses did.

Two-thirds of Americans polled said the tiny house was the home of their dreams, as compared with only about one-fifth that aspired to luxury living.

What's even more surprising is the preference for back-to-nature, tiny-house living held up across all demographic segments – age, gender, race, education, political party, liberal/conservative/moderate, region, urban dwellers and not, income, employment, creative class, marital status, sexual preference, children in home, religion, church attendance, NRA membership and NASCAR – the very identities that define the hot button issues in today's culture wars.

The "Tiny-House Movement" is more than a television show

Zogby says, "As long as all things digital become further intertwined with our lives, more will long for a return to basics." He goes on to explain the cause of the shift:

"My polls were showing that about 1/3 of adults worked at jobs that paid less than the previous, but were finding inner peace by attaining less stuff, and through seeking authentic experience. At the same time, there were Americans who had achieved material success and found themselves not fulfilled – just as baby boomers were finding it was time for a second act in their lives. I called this phenomenon 'secular spiritualism.'"

My work with the affluent consumers, i.e., those who have achieved the material success that Zogby speaks of, mirrors Zogby's American dream home findings.

In a Unity Marketing study with HENRY millennials who've attained post-graduate education and were pursuing career paths that will lead to very high levels of income (e.g., tech, engineering, healthcare, business, etc.). These young affluents, expressed aspirations for a more meaningful, personally richer and rewarding lifestyle, including a more modest-sized home, but with a twist.

Young HENRYs express aspirations for a more meaningful, personally-richer and rewarding lifestyle, including a more modest-sized home.

In an exercise where they created a montage of their American Dream, nearly every one pictured an average suburban home as their housing ideal, complete with white picket fence and a dog in the yard. But they invariably also included a vacation home, on the beach or in the mountains, where they could escape the stress of their demanding careers to get back-to-nature and find contentment missing from their day-to-day lives.

The implications of Zogby's most recent poll go much further than the housing market, though clearly it has greatest relevance to home builders, land developers, realtors, designers, landscapers, the many manufacturers and suppliers serving the home market, as well as mortgage lenders.

Design for living a meaningful life

First is a desire for smaller, more practical and functional homes, designed not for show but for how people really live and want to live. Where once the value of a home was measured largely in square footage, the Tiny House movement establishes a new yardstick for people's quality of life.

Smaller homes but equipped with better-quality appointments save people time, save money, save energy and provide people a different perspective to evaluate new purchases, e.g., what has to go to make room for this new thing I'm considering buying? It makes for mindful consumption that is more considered and more conscientious. It shifts the focus from having more to doing more.

More on Designing the Next Generation's Home

In choosing an ideal tiny home set in nature, not in some artificial planned community, people are craving a lifestyle that is green, clean and healthful. A new study by Ogilvy Health & Wellness Practice explains the need. "Our modern world is at odds with the way we evolved. The 'ape within us' – the primal parts of the brain designed to keep us alive – cannot cope with this new environment."

The wellness movement with its connection to the

back-to-nature trend "is a way for us to manage our modern condition. On one level it is an antidote to toxic stress," the Ogilvy report declares. The simple fact is nature nurtures and that is what the Zogby poll reveals.

People's need to be in touch with nature has implications for developers and builders and how they situate houses; outdoor living brands that provide the furniture, accessories and accoutrements that an outdoor lifestyle requires; interior and landscape design; garden centers and nurseries.

Downsizing of the American home

Tiny House, Big Living proclaims HGTV and this is the trend that Zogby's poll identifies. While people can argue that the square footage of the average new American home has grown dramatically over the last 40+ years, from 1,660 square feet in 1973 to 2,640 in 2016, the latest data also shows a 1.7 percent decline in size from 2015 to 2016, according to the American Housing Survey. This may not seem like much, but it may be the tipping point to the start of an important trend.

We will continue to see a downward shift in the average square footage of new homes, along with growing demand for smaller homes in the resale market. This will be caused by more demand among baby boomers and increasingly among maturing GenXers, the leading edge of which is 53 years of age, for more livable, manageable homes suited to their active, empty-nesting lifestyles, along with reduced demand for family homes on a grand scale among millennials who are giving birth to fewer children, if having children at all.

A sea change is coming to the U.S. housing market and businesses that build those homes, furnish those homes, and provide services to people living in those homes, need to take heed.

From "Old Luxury" to "New Luxury"

Luxury Market Is Evolving

American luxury consumers, the richest and most empowered consumers in the world, not to mention the most numerous, are experiencing an uneasy sense of déjà vu. "It's feeling a lot like 2007," says Cara David, managing partner at research firm YouGov, reporting the results of its Affluent Perspective Global Study among 5,000 of the top 10 percent of consumers around the world.

U.S. consumers comprised the largest segment in the survey with a sample of 2,700. To qualify they needed incomes over $150,000, within the HENRYs range that starts at about $100,000. Overall their mean income was $330,000 and they reported assets of over $3 million. The survey was conducted in the first quarter 2018.

Across the world, there is a rapidly growing base of consumers who can afford luxury and who actively participate in the luxury market. From 2017 to 2018, the participation of the affluent consumers in luxury purchases rose from 67 percent to 71 percent globally. U.S.

consumers are slightly behind the rest of the world, but still their participation in the luxury market grew, with 64 percent purchasing luxury in 2017 and 68 percent in 2018.

This corresponds to the rapid increase in the number of people in the wealth class. Overall YouGov reports there are 15.4 million U.S. households with wealth of $1 million or more, with the wealthiest with assets of $10 million or more growing by 150 percent from 2011-2017. Further there are about 17.1 million U.S. households with incomes over $150,000, accounting for 13.6 percent of total U.S. households.

Enthusiasm to spend on luxury is declining

But despite the growth in the number of people who have the means to buy luxury, there is a significantly lower share of affluents who plan to spend more on luxury in the coming year worldwide – but most especially in the U.S.

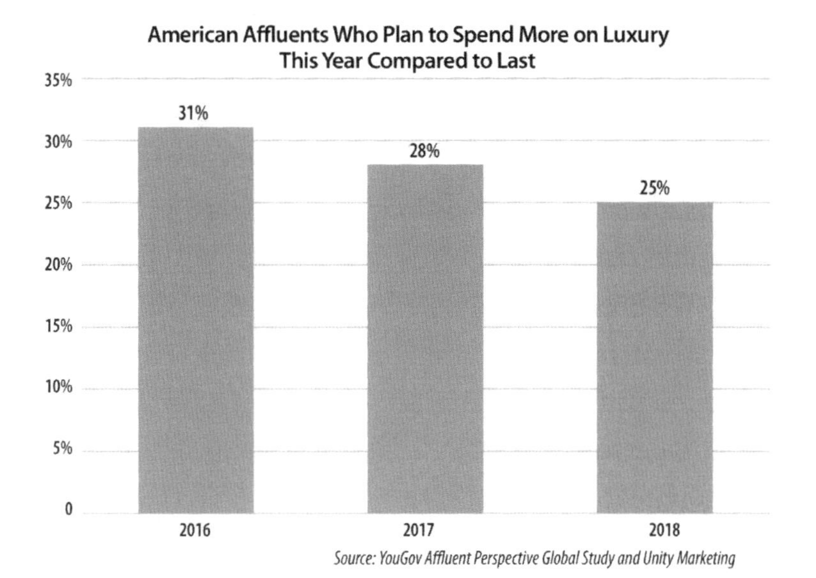

In 2018 only 25 percent of American affluents expect to spend more on luxury, as compared with 31 percent in 2016, a statistically significant difference.

Commenting on the results, Chandler Mount, VP, Affluent Perspective at YouGov, explains, "There are two forces going on. While there is a growing wealth class, at the same time there is an emotional pull-back. They don't feel as confident as they could or they did in the past."

However, this doesn't necessarily mean doom and gloom for luxury brands since there are more affluent people that can afford to indulge in luxury. The growing numbers of affluents can make up for reduced spending at the personal level, but he cautions, "We might see an increase in the luxury market, but it is going to be harder to get."

Economic uncertainty is taking the wind out of their sails

The chief factor putting the brakes on American luxury consumer spending is their lack of confidence in the world's and the nation's economy. This is where the sense of déjà vu is coming from.

"This well-informed, educated group was impacted one way or another by the Great Recession," Cara David says. "We believe this pull-back in spending is a result of a variety of reasons, primarily their concern for the U.S. economic future."

On a personal level, affluent Americans feel they have their own house in order, with 54 percent reporting confidence in their personal economies and their saving rate is at a healthy 25 percent. But, David notes, their concern over retirement assets continues to grow, rising from 43 percent in 2017 to 51 percent in 2018.

The net effect of restrained luxury spending will translate into a -3 percent change in interest in purchasing luxury globally in the nine major categories of goods and services the survey tracks. But in the U.S. that downward trajectory drops even further, to -7 percent.

For the U.S. market, David predicts a pull back in most every category, with jewelry/watches and fashion impacted the most. "This disciplined approach in spending, combined with other factors disrupting the luxury sector, will make for a very competitive marketplace," she warns.

"Changes in Latitude, Changes in Attitude"

In tracing the trajectory of consumers' attitudes toward luxury indulgence since 2002, the study identifies four key pivot points. In 2002 the luxury consumers had an overpowering conspicuous-consumption drive which came to an abrupt end with the recession. "In 2007 it hit them like a ton of bricks," says Mount. "They bought too many houses, too much stuff to put in them, and too many cars. Resourcefulness, simplification and comparison shopping became the name of the game."

Then in 2012 as the economy got stronger and consumers felt more confident in their jobs, luxury consumers' mood turned from saving money toward getting the most value out of the purchases they made.

"The search was on for how to spend money for the best stuff. It became a drive for quality, craftsmanship and service provided by a brand to justify the price that they would spend. It didn't return to a question of, 'How do I buy more houses and fill them with more stuff?', but 'How do I buy the best stuff I possibly can?'" he says.

In 2018 this mindset has continued to evolve beyond just a search for quality, craftsmanship and service, to looking for purchases that give more meaning. "They are looking for brands that serve a higher purpose, that reinforce and mirror their personal values," Mount explains.

A search for deeper meaning

They call it a trend toward "Goodness-based spending." Overall 4 out of 10 affluent decision makers see that luxury brands have very similar quality and craftsmanship. What they want now is brands that express values in line with their personal values. "It is a search for deeper meaning," David says.

The affluents hold most dear the values of honesty, being relatable, committed to doing the right thing, sharing their personal values and following sustainable practices in the brands with which they choose to align. A decisive 71 percent of luxury consumers surveyed said, "I am looking to connect with brands that make a positive impact on the world."

"Luxury consumers are searching for stability and security in a world where things are unstable and security is questioned," David says. "They value inner peace for a number of reasons, one of which is finding their place on the right side of an unbalanced world."

Luxury consumers are looking for brands with a higher purpose. They want their purchases to help them attain their ultimate personal goals, which, in the survey, include being healthier, spending more time with family, going to new places and doing new things, learning something new, to be a better person, and to simplify life.

Luxury consumers are looking for brands with a higher purpose.

For the affluents their relationship with brands has become very personal. They want to engage with brands that are a mirror of themselves and their personal values. Exceptional quality, craftsmanship and service are simply table stakes. "They are looking for brand perfection, to be flawless," David concludes. "Their high standards have to be luxury brands' high standards."

Redesigning Luxury in a Brand New Style

The changes that HENRY millennials are bringing to the luxury market demand that brands redesign their luxury in a new style. Brands must reimagine, refit and align their luxury to these new ideas and perceptions of what luxury is and where it fits into their lifestyle now and in the future.

De Beers, the diamond industry leader, is undertaking such an effort in launching a new type of diamond – one grown in a laboratory, for a new type of customer – the self-purchasing HENRY woman.

CASE STUDY: De Beers

Lab-grown diamonds are now a girl's best friend

Look at any list of the most powerful advertising messages of all times and the 1948 De Beers-N.W. Ayers slogan "A Diamond Is Forever" is at the top. While many claim the line made the $80 billion diamond industry what it is today, advertising didn't do it alone.

The diamond's allure was further propelled in the early 1950s by the seductive image of Marilyn Monroe singing an ode to the stones:

Men grow cold as girls grow old
And we all lose our charms in the end.
But square-cut or pear-shaped
These rocks don't lose their shape.
Diamonds are a girl's best friend.

Marilyn would have been 92 years old on June 1, 2018, and she never lived long enough to experience the truth in those lyrics. But her image and that song reinforced the "A Diamond Is Forever" message in a deep cultural way that no paid advertising ever could have achieved.

Fast forward to today and a hot new rock is threatening the genuine diamond-is-forever concept: laboratory-grown diamonds. Thanks to advances in manufacturing technology, gemstone-quality diamonds can now be industrially grown. These lab-grown diamonds are identical in composition and structure to diamonds formed naturally over the ages in the earth.

Priced lower than natural diamonds and brought to market without the collateral environmental and human damage associated with mining operations, lab-grown diamonds are increasingly the choice for the conscientious, social justice, values-focused consumer.

No consumer is more conscientious or values-focused than HENRY millennials.

And no consumer is more conscientious or values-focused than 18-to-38-year-old HENRY millennials, who are the primary target for the diamond industry's flagship product: engagement rings.

Diamonds disrupted

As of yet, the lab-grown diamond industry is tiny compared to mined diamonds, representing less than 1 percent of the global market for rough diamonds, according to estimates by Morgan Stanley. But that is about to change.

"The introduction of hot-forged jewelry-grade diamonds, identical to those the earth takes eons to mete out, has sweeping implications for the $80 billion industry that has relied on the perceived scarcity of mined diamonds to drive up value," said Amish Shah, president of R.A. Riam Group which offers mined-diamond jewelry, and ALTR Created Diamonds selling the lab-grown variety.

"Sales of lab-created diamonds, now estimated at $150 million, are expected to increase to $1 billion by 2020 and outpace mined diamonds, which have been in decline," Shah says.

Until now the mined-diamond industry – and De Beers – have been pushing back against the disruptive lab-grown producers with the claim that only mined diamonds are the real thing. Lab-grown are fake pretenders. But that argument doesn't hold water.

"Lab-created diamonds and earth-mined diamonds are exactly the same thing. It's like ice on a frozen lake and ice created in your freezer. One is created by a natural process and one by a manmade process. But in the end, they are identical in all ways down to the atomic level," said Gary LaCourt, CEO of Forever Companies that markets alternative and lab-grown diamond brands Diamond Nexus, 1215 Diamond, and Forever Artisans.

De Beers sees the writing on the wall

No company stands to lose more than De Beers, which controls 35–40 percent of the mined-diamond market. After years of disavowing the authenticity of lab-grown diamonds, De Beers has done a 180-degree about face and just announced it is launching a line of man-made diamonds under the Lightbox Jewelry brand.

"Lightbox will transform the lab-grown diamond

sector by offering consumers a lab-grown product they have told us they want but aren't getting: affordable fashion jewelry that may not be forever, but is perfect for right now," Bruce Cleaver, CEO of DeBeers Group said in a statement. "Our extensive research tells us this is how consumers regard lab-grown diamonds – as a fun, pretty product that shouldn't cost that much – so we see an opportunity that's been missed by lab-grown diamond producers."

Adding to the fun element in the Lightbox Jewelry line will be an emphasis on colored pink and blue stones to compliment the traditional clear white diamonds. Prices will start at $200 for a quarter-carat stone to $800 for one-carat. These prices, however, don't include the cost of the jewelry setting, which will initially include earrings and necklace designs, but not rings.

The company release does not specifically mention the primary target for the Lightbox Jewelry line. It is clearly self-purchasing women, not men buying diamonds for women. Strategically, Lightbox won't threaten DeBeers' core engagement ring market (since it is not even offering rings in the collection). To that end, DeBeers distinguishes its mined-diamond offering as "forever," as in "A Diamond Is Forever," compared to its Lightbox style savvy alternative as "for right now."

It also is a smart move that DeBeers calls Lightbox "fashion jewelry," positioning it as the more affordable alternative to natural, mined-diamond "fine jewelry" quality. The official industry distinction between fine and fashion jewelry is that fashion doesn't have precious gemstones or precious metals (other than plating), while fine jewelry is made with natural precious gemstones and metals.

As DeBeers moves Lightbox Jewelry into the market, it guides its customers: "If you want fashion jewelry, Lightbox is your choice. If you want precious fine jewelry, then Forevermark and DeBeers Jewelers is for you."

Millennial HENRYs want different options

DeBeers may not be able to sell that distinction, however, as millennials have already shown that they aren't buying into the idea that a lab-grown diamond is in any way inferior to its mined counterpart. Quite the contrary.

Millennials want to know the products they buy aren't harming anybody in their production.

Among consumers in general, and millennials specifically, mined-diamonds have a bad reputation for the high human cost and environmental damage that mining operations entail. This generation is fixated on responsible sourcing and manufacturing of the products they buy. Lab-grown diamonds meet that demand, while mined-diamonds fall short.

"Millennials want to know that the products they buy aren't harming anybody in their production. This is across all consumer products," said Marty Hurwitz, CEO of

MVI Marketing, whose company recently conducted a study among 1,000+ American consumers, aged 21–40, across all income ranges with half having household incomes of $50,000 or higher.

"That's why companies are tracing chain of custody and providing transparency of supply chain. There isn't a product in Whole Foods, Nordstrom or Walmart, for that matter, that isn't being traced in case someone asks. Millennials are driving this trend," Hurwitz says.

In that survey, nearly 70 percent of consumers said "Yes," they would consider a lab-grown diamond for the center stone in an engagement ring if they were shopping or shopping with someone for an engagement ring. That represents an increase of 13 percentage points in only one year. "Millennials are telling the jewelry industry this is a product they are interested in and will come into the store to look at it," Hurwitz adds.

De Beers moves to control the diamond narrative

By embracing lab-grown diamonds, De Beers is disrupting the industry's stance against the numerous startups eating away at their market dominance. These brands include **Ada Diamonds**, **ALTR Created Diamonds**, **Diamond Foundry**, **New Dawn Diamonds** and **Pure Grown** among others, though no market-share leader has emerged as yet.

Rather than fight the rising tide against laboratory-grown diamonds which has found a consumer market ready, willing, and able to embrace it, De Beers is getting in early to take a leadership position in an emerging category with no clear-cut leader. Now it will have one, with De Beers' mighty marketing muscle moving in to define the category and establish its positioning against the lab-grown upstarts, as well as elevating its mined-diamond precious jewelry offering.

De Beers helped make diamonds what they are today. Next, De Beers is going to try to make laboratory-diamonds what they will be tomorrow: a fun fashion pretender to the real, rare, precious, natural, "forever" diamond.

And as it did with diamonds throughout its 130-year history, De Beers is aiming to become the market leader by using its power to establish prices for both the mined and laboratory-diamond markets.

Its Lightbox Jewelry prices are way below current levels in the industry today, and given advances in technology and production processes, the costs to produce manmade stones will only continue to fall. By establishing a low-price alternative to the real thing, De Beers will aim to drive up the prices for its natural stones. It's a very smart and bold move and one that few saw coming.

HENRYs Are Gatekeepers to the Future Luxury Market

Understanding HENRYs Is the Key

The middle class isn't the middle class any longer, now that the bottom has fallen out of the discretionary spending power of the middle-income customers. If a brand traditionally targeted middle-class, middle-income consumers, like **Walmart** and **Ikea**, then the HENRYs are the new target customer. However, they are poorly understood by many brands that traditionally sell to the masses.

What's more, HENRYs are important to luxury brands because most everyone who reaches Ultra-affluent income levels starts out as a HENRY. And shopping habits learned while people are living as HENRYs often carry over into their later stages of life. HENRYs, because they are smart and exceedingly effective shoppers, have learned how to live a lifestyle several rungs up the income ladder simply by making smart choices when they shop.

HENRYs are the most important new demographic

consumer segment in today's post-recession economy and the key to marketing and retailing success. They are the new middle-class customer for mass marketers and the gatekeepers for the future luxury consumer market.

If retailers and marketers aim to draw more HENRY affluents, with their significantly greater spending power over middle-income consumers, they need to combine strategies borrowed from high-end brands, along with more mass-market tactics to send a clear message that these high-potential customers are understood, respected, and catered to.

HENRYs are the most important new demographic consumer segment in today's post-recession economy and the key to marketing and retailing success.

Specifically, mass-marketing strategies must focus on value, so that the HENRYs see they get a greater return on their spending investment. Meanwhile, the luxury-focused strategies are directed to delivering high quality goods and services, including careful attention to superior materials and workmanship, and making customers feel pride of ownership for the items bought, as well as pride of belonging to a cadre of shoppers that are smart and in the know. That is the strategy that Shinola has so successfully used.

While the purchases of the upper class (mansions, yachts, etc.) may garner far more media attention, their small population translates into a smaller, significantly more nuanced market. However, there is a much larger market merely one notch down – upper-middle class (i.e., the HENRYs) rather than the true upper class (the Ultras, the high-net-worth and Ultra-high-net-worth wealthy). These are households with both means and aspirations for an affluent lifestyle; however, achieving that often requires sacrifices in overall household consumption.

➲ OPPORTUNITY: New Luxury

How to get HENRYs to spend more?

A new study from Deloitte, the international consulting and financial advisory firm, helps unravel the prevailing mystery of how to market luxury to the new generation luxury consumers.

Entitled "Bling it on: What makes a millennial spend more," it studied millennials specifically and their attitudes and purchase motivations in the luxury market based upon a survey with over 1,000 millennials, aged 20–30 years, in the U.S., U.K., Italy and China who expressed an interest in luxury spending. While this study focused on millennials, its findings are especially relevant to young HENRYs, since these are the consumers who have the means (i.e., income) and the motivations (i.e., all these consumers expressed an interest in luxury) to trade up to luxury.

Many of the findings were not unexpected, such as their willingness to purchase luxury goods online and the influence of social media and brand websites as a source of information to propel their luxury purchases. But one finding popped for me:

Over one-fourth of the American millennials report no luxury purchases of $500 or more in the last 12 months, whereas the survey average was only 16 percent. There is a huge gap between American millennials and those in the other markets in their willingness to indulge in high-end purchases.

Bridging the luxury gap with American HENRYs

This finding has significant implications for luxury brands marketing in America because consumers' past purchase behavior is a good predictor of future behavior. If 26 percent of millennials who are interested in luxury goods haven't purchased any recently, it certainly doesn't bode well for the future of luxury brands in the U.S., the world's largest luxury market, as reported by the Bain Luxury Study.

The U.S. also leads the world in the number of affluent consumers. Credit Suisse reports that in 2017 there were 15.4 million Americans with $1 million or more in wealth – or approximately 8 percent of American adults. The other top 10 countries for millionaires combined have fewer than in America – 15.2 million millionaires.

In Unity Marketing's in-depth "Millennials on the Road to Affluence" study, which included both qualitative and quantitative research, we studied young people's attitudes about luxury. Our qualitative sample was a select group of HENRY millennials having post-graduate educational levels and who are pursuing careers that will lead to high incomes, such as law, medicine and health, engineering, tech and business. One of the respondents said "Luxury is nothing but a marketers' label," which he said meant it was overpriced.

American millennials trailed far behind the other markets in their purchases of high-end fashion or luxury goods.

The millennial HENRYs are smart shoppers who know how to use all the tools at their disposal to find the best value when shopping.

While the Deloitte study shows millennials are most motivated in their purchases by quality, followed by uniqueness, the brand name, its ethics and image did not particularly motivate them when comparing a luxury versus a more affordable alternative. Applying the descriptor "luxury" to a particular brand may well turn these young people off more than it turns them on when it comes to attracting their attention and getting them to buy.

What luxury brands are selling may not be what millennial HENRYs are buying

It is a mistake to assume that the millennial generation will aspire to the same luxury as previous generations. This generation, thanks to the internet and how it has pulled back the curtain revealing the marketing strategies on which the allure of luxury brands are built, are discovering they can acquire luxury-quality goods at significantly lower prices.

Status symbols as represented by luxury brands don't have the same meaning for millennials. They still value status, but for them it is status defined by who they are and what they have achieved, not how much money they spent buying some overly-expensive luxury brand.

As a result, a gap is growing between what the customers believe luxury to be and what the industry thinks it is, as discovered in the most recent "State of Luxury" study conducted among 600 luxury industry executives by Unity Marketing and *Luxury Daily*, the world's leading luxury business publication. The opportunity for renewed luxury industry growth lies in bridging that perception gap, as this luxury insider shared, "There is an opportunity for luxury brands to re-examine their roots and rethink their offerings and messaging to reflect what the consumer is looking for."

Shifts in the demographics and mindset of today's luxury consumers have brought about profound changes in the way they shop and buy and how luxury fits into their lifestyle. Not to mention new competitors are fast and furiously emerging and are not bound by the traditions prevalent in the luxury industry – those same traditions that hamper established brands in this increasingly disrupted luxury market.

Luxury Is a State of Mind, not a Brand or a Price Point

Millennials still want luxury, but luxury must be consistent with their personal values. Here are some ideas for luxury brands to get back on track with the emerging millennial generation HENRY customers:

Out with "Old Luxury," in with "New Luxury"

The traditional ideas about luxury as aspirational or a status symbol, which have been an important element in marketing and positioning many heritage luxury brands in the past, have taken on a negative taint in a cultural climate that demonizes the excesses of the rich and wealthy. Say the word "luxury" and negative, rather than positive images, are evoked, like conspicuous consumption, indulgence, exclusivity, elitism, extravagance, status seeking, and income inequality.

What's more, other positive values that luxury brands have traditionally filled – quality, style, workmanship, design – are increasingly being satisfied by premium and lower-priced brands, or challenger brands as Deloitte describes them: "It is no accident that most successful challenger brands in the industry have their roots in digital and/or social media marketing aimed at millennial consumers."

This calls on luxury brands to downplay the negative connotations associated with luxury and play up the positive attributes of luxury in a brand new style and through brand new mediums. Brands must find ways to make their luxury relevant to HENRY millennials, not just using luxury as a label they should aspire to own but to convey true meaning and value to the customers.

E-Commerce is essential

Many luxury brands were surprised by the rapid rise of the digital age. While many understand the power of the internet, usually as a branding and marketing tool, too few have fully embraced the concept of omni-channel strategies.

"The great challenge for brand owners seeking to capture millennials is how to communicate to a generation with shifting preferences and loose brand loyalties, and for whom no single channel appears to predominate," Deloitte writes. "Yet amid this apparent uncertainty, the one factor that plays a role in almost every aspect of millennial consumption is the rise of online."

The internet has changed how customers get information and how they make purchasing decisions. A powerful e-commerce presence is no longer optional for luxury brands. But the Deloitte report stresses that "Online sales alone do not capture the full significance of the rise of online interaction."

Luxury brands' heritage and tradition has given way to immediacy and now.

Due to the rise of the digital world, luxury brands' heritage and tradition has given way to immediacy and now. That is a critical component of the new luxury that today's internet-savvy customers demand.

Tell new brand stories that millennials can share

One of the more interesting findings in the Deloitte study is the profound influence that millennials' friends play in their luxury leanings, especially among American millennials. When asked which of these three choices have the greatest influence on their purchase decisions – a friend they admire, the brand, or a favorite celebrity or influencer – 39 percent of American millennials say their friends have the dominant role, as compared with 27 percent among the survey average.

Further, Deloitte found that millennials don't have the brand loyalty that previous generations have embraced. The largest share, 36 percent, say they will buy what they like regardless of brand. They are more than willing to pay attention to brands with new stories to tell that are more aligned with their personal values and the values of their social circle. This is how new emerging luxury brands have gained traction with this generation. These challenger brands talk to the millennials in ways that are more meaningful and valuable to them.

So for example, they are attuned to luxury brands that are more inclusive, rather than exclusive, but that also can be individualized or personalized, like **Interior Define** in home furnishings or **Knot Standard** in men's fashion.

They want luxury that is self-expressive, and not self-absorbed or narcissistic. Compare **Louis Vuitton**'s monogram canvas tote bags, which may be the world's biggest perpetrator of logo pollution, with **Everlane**'s understated, but equally functional 100 percent leather tote for only $175. Everlane is the epitome of a new luxury brand, positioned as "luxury basics for less," that the company delivers thanks to a commitment to "radical transparency" in pricing and ethical, conscientious manufacturing.

HENRYs want luxury that is democratic, not elitist and reserved only for the 1 percent, like **Shinola** and its watch for presidents that most every American can afford to own and wear. And they crave luxury that is authentic and made for them, not some celebrity, like **Canada Goose** jackets which are functionally designed to keep their owners warm, whether worn by a super model or the man or woman in the streets of New York or Chicago.

In conclusion, a rising tide of millennial wealth could result in a new luxury boom starting in the middle of the next decade, but only if brands meet this new generation with luxuries that reflect their values and world view. However, if luxury brands keep doing what they've always done, putting status before substance, they will miss the mark. The world has changed and luxury brands must change with it.

OPPORTUNITY: Online

Marketing to HENRYs future revealed in five online brands

Online is the next frontier for marketing to HENRYs. It's where brands can find their next path to growth, but for a variety of reasons luxury brands have been notoriously slow to follow it. For an industry steeped in heritage and tradition, change doesn't come naturally, but in today's dynamically changing consumer market, that is exactly what luxury brands must do.

While luxury brands have accepted that they must market online, they have been much slower to accept that they must sell there as well. That remains the stumbling block.

"A big part of luxury brands' hesitance to embrace sales online has been how to keep that luxury aspect of the brand, if it is so easily available," says Lori Mitchell-Keller, Global General Manager, Consumer Industries at SAP. "Keeping that perceived cachet of luxury in the online world have made them slow to migrate there."

But migrate sales online is what they have to do for a prosperous future. Bain & Company recently reported online luxury sales growth is phenomenal, increasing by 24 percent in 2017. Yet it still accounts for only 9 percent of the total personal luxury goods market worldwide.

On the surface online's less than 10-percent market share might not seem compelling, but the industry's perception may not match the consumers' reality. Compare that meager market share with luxury consumers' preferences in where they like to shop and a totally different picture emerges.

Luxury brands will lose share if they are not able to interact in the way the world is changing.

In a global survey of affluent consumers with annual incomes of $150,000 per year, or equivalent, the Luxury Institute found that 21 percent of those surveyed prefer to shop luxury online, and another 27 percent had no preference between online or in-store shopping. A near majority of luxury consumers don't shy away from shopping online, rather they actively embrace it.

"Luxury brands will lose share if they are not able to interact in the way the world is changing and the way customers want to interact with them," Mitchell-Keller maintains.

While heritage luxury brands drag their feet, plenty of others are jumping in unburdened by fears of losing their luxe on the internet. "We are seeing a lot of luxury brands being created online, companies like **Farfetch**,

Net-a-Porter, Bonobos, that have much more of an online than physical presence," Mitchell-Keller says. "And other more traditional brands, like **Badgley Mischka** and **Gucci**, have figured out how to create, maintain, even enhance their luxe cachet online. There is no secret or easy answer how they've been able to do that, but it can and is being done."

Two of these born on the internet brands, she notes, have recently been acquired by other companies – Yoox Net-a-Porter by Richemont, and Bonobos by Walmart – and Farfetch signed deals with Fendi, Burberry, and Chanel in advance of an expected IPO.

Such deals are expected to pick up in the future, as Mitchell-Keller explains, "The main reason physical luxury brands are acquiring digital brands is because they haven't figured out the online equation yet. They are looking for help to reach the digital customer."

Putting our heads together, we think these 5 brands best exemplify the future of luxury online.

Farfetch goes further

Founded in 2008 as an online luxury fashion platform, **Farfetch** is seamlessly blending in-store access to fashions across the globe with internet convenience. With offices in 11 fashion hubs, from which it offers same-day express delivery, it lists products from over 700 boutiques and fashion brands. It carries a multitude of heritage and emerging designer brands, including Dolce & Gabbana, Givenchy, and Chloé.

Having acquired the London-based **Browns** boutique in 2015, it used that platform to introduce its technology-enhanced "Store of the Future" concept that marries the digital and personal experience luxury shoppers desire.

Given its chops in digital luxury marketing, Farfetch also initiated a white label digital service called "Farfetch Black and White" for brands that want to use its platform to power their own branded online presence.

Numerous heritage brands are coming on board in one way or another, including **Burberry** to list all inventory in its marketplace, **Fendi** for customized handbags, **Gucci** for 90-minute delivery service, and most recently **Chanel**.

But tellingly, Chanel was quick to point out that its Farfetch partnership will not include selling fashion online, rather using its proprietary in-store technology for physical retail. "We are not starting to sell Chanel on the Farfetch marketplace – I want to be very clear on that," said Chanel's president of fashion Bruno Pavlovky in announcing the deal. To which Mitchell-Keller asks, "How much share will they lose while they are trying to figure online out?"

Such reluctance to embrace full-on digital access for customers is indicative of an industry attitude that has to change to ensure a vibrant future. It is ridiculous for a brand like Chanel to force its 21st century customers to shop like they did in the 1980s.

Net-a-Porter brings it

Just acquired by **Richemont** following a merger with

YOOX in 2015, Net-a-Porter, founded in 2000, takes a more heavily content-driven strategy than its closest competitor, Farfetch. But like Farfetch it offers white-label digital support to designer brands through its YNAP platform which Richemont says will continue to operate as a separate entity. Nonetheless, it will make strange bedfellows, since YNAP operates flagship online stores for many competitive **Kering** brands, including Bottega Veneta, Balenciaga, and YSL.

While Mitchell-Keller admires Net-a-Porter, she thinks its Outnet website that offers discounted fashions in flash-sale format is especially in tune with how the next generation wants to shop. "My son, who is totally a millennial, had me log on to order a pair of gold Nike shoes, which I understand are status items for the college crowd. So here we are logged in at midnight for the countdown and find out we are #500 in line to order. It is such a different experience than I am used to where luxury brands pamper you in the store, but millennials don't necessarily want that. They want this," she says.

Outnet makes it fun for millennials. It is fast, it's limited, it's accessible, and it's cheaper.

Bonobos shows men how to wear it

Bonobos is one of those born on the internet luxury brands, or near-luxury for those who want to quibble, that have captured the loyalty of affluent men shoppers, a hard demographic to attract into the store. It's achieved that by not just selling clothes, but showing men how to dress fashionably. It is also helped by offering casual-luxe styles that modern men favor.

"I'm intrigued by the way Bonobos shows their clothes," says Mitchell-Keller. "It's not just a guy standing there like on most websites. You can see the movement and men interacting with each other. It is a much different experience than just going online and seeing picture after picture of clothes. It's engaging."

As a result, Bonobos caught the eye of a big company suitor, Walmart, which acquired the company last year, and with it a thought-leader in the next generation of retail fashion, Andy Dunn who joins another e-commerce powerhouse, Marc Lore, at Walmart to give it a leg up into new internet markets.

Badgley Mischka dresses its models with tech

While the **Badgley Mischka** brand has long maintained a vibrant online e-commerce presence, co-owner and co-designer James Mischka is described by Mitchell-Keller as a "technology geek." Being as attuned to tech as fashion, he partnered with SAP to create a runway app for a New York Fashion Week where those in the audience could vote on each look as it walked down the runway. "In 9 minutes they got feedback that usually takes them 6 months to get," she says.

The results were eye opening. The company discovered that a dress they hadn't thought would make much of a splash turned out to be the #2 most popular look. This allowed the company to place sufficient orders to get it into the stores in record time.

The audience in turn loved the ability to get all the fashion details on their phones instantaneously. The models, who were back stage reading the results and competing to see whose look scored highest, loved it. And the other designers at the show were envious and lined up afterwards to get an app for their next runway show.

Thinking about new ways consumers can interact and engage with a luxury brand is what makes Badgley Mischka an important luxury brand for the future.

"Too many luxury brands aren't thinking about the technology. They are thinking about product, which is important, but they have to understand how their brand is being consumed differently than it used to be consumed," Mitchell-Keller notes.

Gucci breaks out of the luxury culture

And we can't finish our look at luxury online without mentioning **Gucci**. In an interview on CNBC, **Kering**'s chairman and CEO Francois-Henri Pinault said its Gucci brand is doing about 50 percent of its sales with millennials. In recognition of its online success, L2 Research, which specializes in data-driven analysis, gave its top spot for best performing digital fashion brand to Gucci in 2016 and 2017.

Gucci has broken out of the inbred, digitally-adverse culture that plagues so many other luxury brands.

Time is money

In conclusion, Mitchell-Keller and I see a whole digital transformation that is going to happen in luxury, just as it has happened in other markets. While we recognize that the experience of in-store shopping, and the pampering luxury consumers can find there, isn't going to be replaced by digital engagement, customers today value the luxury of convenience that online delivers too.

"The time issue is a huge one," Mitchell-Keller concludes. "It's not just that everyone is now on social media. Everybody also has huge demands on their time. It's a very different world than 20 years ago when these brands started to become popular. Luxury brands have to adapt to the way that consumers want to interact with their product now, and that increasingly is going to be online."

New Luxury Marketing for HENRYs

Out with the Old, In with the New

In 2013, the American Marketing Association changed the definition of marketing. It went from the old 4Ps definition which most of us practicing marketers were drilled in: Product, Price, Promotion, Placement, to a new one based upon the idea of value:

> Marketing is the activity, set of institutions, and processes for creating, communicating, delivering, and exchanging offerings that have *value* for customers, clients, partners, and society at large.

Judging from the sorry state of business today – the record number of retail closings in 2017 and 2018 the most recent example – most marketers never got the "memo," or if they did, they gave lip service to it, but kept on doing marketing the way they always have done it.

Today's marketers must answer to a higher calling, one that truly reflects the changing mindset, expectations and needs of customers. This is even more important for marketers aiming at the young HENRYs, as they are on the cutting-edge in the search for value and meaning in the consumer goods and services they purchase.

A case in point: luxury brands continue to believe that the way to market is by creating "aspiration" for the brand – the hope or ambition that acquiring the brand will enable the HENRY customer to achieve some special status or position.

But I've got news for those brands: Aspirational marketing may work for some people, but not those who can actually afford what the luxe brands are selling. The HENRY consumers aren't really interested in status and position. They don't need any brand to give it to them.

Luxury marketing must evolve from its focus on "aspiration" to one of "inspiration."

Luxury marketing needs to evolve from its focus on "aspiration" to one of "inspiration." It's about inspiring the HENRYs to see how the brand is meaningful and delivers a measurable value that enhances their lifestyle. Here's how:

Marketing to HENRYs in a brand new style

Education and training aside, one reason we cling to the old 4Ps of marketing is its simplicity. Following that model for simplicity, Ogilvy & Mather's Brian Fetherstonhaugh has proposed a new formula, the 4Es: Experience, Everyplace, Exchange, and Evangelism. The secret is to use these 4E ideas to communicate and deliver meaningful value to the customer.

Luxury brands, and the customers they serve, are at the pinnacle of the consumer hierarchy. Marketing strategies and tactics based on the 4Ps make a clear statement that the brand is outmoded, old-fashioned, and worse, for the masses. To sell to the contemporary HENRY affluents, luxury marketers need to use the 4Es.

Experiences Replace Product

We all talk about the experiential economy and it's easy to market a brand when it's an experience, like dining, travel, or spas. But what about all the luxury goods brands. How do they turn their products into an experience for the customer? Yes, customer service is important, but it takes more than that.

In order to turn luxury goods products into experiences for the customer, companies need to do a deep dive into understanding the feelings that drive customers to make a purchase, and no 'big data' or quantitative data can provide that answer. It requires getting up close and personal with the customers to understand the special experiences they get from the brand and its products.

Brands that understand this new experiential dimension in the marketing formula include **Stitch Fix** and **Trunk Club**, both of which put a personal stylist to work to select complete outfits according to the woman's or man's style profile and deliver care packages to try on in the privacy and comfort of one's home.

Or **Laudi Vidni** which involves the customer in the creation of their personal handbag, specifying the style, leather, lining and do-dads to create their own personal design.

Or **Project Gravitas** which started with a simple idea, giving women the perfect LBD (little black dress) designed to enhance her own body shape, with the added confidence of a shapewear lining so that she always looks her best.

All these brands turn the chore of shopping and buying into a personal experience for the customer.

CASE STUDY: Apple

How Apple has evolved in the experience economy

For the latest and greatest in personal technology, everybody looks to **Apple**. They lead the pack in creating innovative, user-friendly computing products. And the company takes the same innovative, forward-looking approach to retail.

Yet people think of Apple as a product-first technology company, when in fact it is a hybrid that seamlessly combines products and services into a new kind of company that is ideally suited to the evolving experience economy. It transforms its products into experiences and delivers those product experiences through a new kind of retailing model that elevates the Apple Stores from a place to buy things into a destination to have meaningful, important experiences.

As innovative as Apple is as a product company, it is equally innovative as a retailer. That's why retailers across the board need to listen and learn from Apple. But my experience is that unless you're a retailer that competes in Apple's vertical, like **Verizon** and **Best Buy**, what Apple is doing at retail is not really on your radar, unless it is as a customer.

With so many struggling retailers trying to respond effectively to the emerging experience economy, retailers in every vertical can learn from Apple. Here are three important lessons about its experience-based retail business model that Apple has implemented and retailers across the board from grocery, fashion, home and the rest need to understand too:

Become a place to learn

In the experience economy, consumers take very seriously, and seem to enjoy, their experiences leading up to a purchase. In research with consumers, I am amazed how much time, effort and consideration these time-starved, multi-tasking people devote to pre-purchase research for purchases both large and small. They are relentless in gathering all the information they can about buying the things that matter to them, and it seems so many things matter.

Marketers have an awesome opportunity to provide the information their customers crave. But the secret is not pushing that information out as a marketing ploy, but to use the information to draw customers in. It's got to arouse curiosity and be really meaningful, useful information that will give them an edge, not marketing fluff which they can smell from a mile away.

The secret is not pushing marketing messages out, but using marketing to draw HENRYs in.

"Today at Apple" is its answer to providing meaningful, useful information tailored to the interests and needs of its customers. Sure, a lot of the "Today at Apple" educational programming is aimed at helping its customers learn how to use its technology, but much more importantly, it also exposes them to new experiences in music, art, design and photography, broadening their perspectives and delivering information from subject-matter experts educating and informing them, not shilling Apple products.

Recently I've been working in home furnishings retail and have learned that decorating a livable, comfortable and stylish room is not as easy as portrayed on 30-second Wayfair commercials. Retail home furnishings customers are eager to learn more about home design. A furniture or home furnishings retailer should be a place where consumers get that information, so that they can become better designers of their home space and better home furnishings consumers.

The same thinking applies to any other category of retail, including fashion, grocery, gifts, books, jewelry, beauty, crafts, office supplies, and pharmacy. Consumers today, the customers retailers hope to serve, are information sponges. Retailers should think beyond providing information just about their merchandise to providing information about the customers' lifestyles and their dreams that the merchandise they sell makes possible.

Meet that higher-level need with meaningful information, above and beyond the lower-level drive to sell more product, and you will bind that customer for life. In the experiential economy, retailers need a similar "Today at Apple" strategy to serve their customers' lifestyle interests, not just their product-specific needs.

Become a place to gather

Now with nearly 500 stores worldwide and after 15 years of retail behind it, Apple is re-envisioning its stores as "Town Squares," places where people can come together, learn and experience, as well as places to buy product. The redesign is more than just window dressing, though it includes that, like adding living trees to the modernistic store design and changing the name of its Genius Bars to "Genius Groves." It transcends the idea of the four walls of the physical store from a place to display products in anticipation of a sale into an environment where people will gather.

"The store becomes one with the community," Angela Ahrendts, Apple's senior vice president of retail explained in an interview with The Verge. "The over-arching vision of the future of Apple retail . . . is what do we want Apple's role in the community to be?" That goal, according to Ahrendts, is to make Apple stores forums for collaboration.

This is a powerful idea: the retailer as a place for people to share experiences in a community of collaboration. "As we need less or want less, stores that figure out how to make you go there – where buying is secondary to the experience, but not the focus of the experience – are going to be important places," Ken Nisch, chairman of retail design firm JGA, shared with me in *Shops that POP!*, as he pointed to both Starbucks and Apple as retailers that do just that.

Retail becomes a place for people to share experiences in a community of collaboration.

"It used to be that lifestyle retail was the ultimate. Now it is concept retail, shops like **American Girl Place** and **Selfridges**," Nisch shared. "These are stores at the top of the retail pyramid that have built a community. They become part of the community."

Malls as they try to figure out how to bring customers back again are beginning to understand the need to become vital members of their communities, not just places for people to buy stuff, but community centers where people come together to share and connect. Main Street USA, and the retailers and other local businesses that make their home there, are places where those community experiences can occur.

Become a place to serve

As retailers go, Apple is the most modern of modern retailers, but one aspect of retail never goes out of style: good old-fashioned customer service. Modeling its customer service approach after luxury hotelier **Ritz-Carlton**'s Steps of Service guidelines, Apple adapted its own steps of service, creating an acronym that appropriately spells A-P-P-L-E:

(A) Approach customers with a personalized warm welcome – "May I help you" is not helpful at all for retail. Retail personnel need a new script that really connects with people and gets them to answer beyond, "No, just looking."

(P) Probe politely to understand customers' needs – The Apple sales philosophy is not to sell, but rather to help customers solve problems. Its stated goal is to "delight the customers." Forbes.com contributor Steve Denning explained, "Apple has grasped that making money is the result of the firm's actions, not the goal. By delighting the customer, Apple ends up making more money than it would if it set out to make money."

(P) **Present** a solution for the customer to take home today – That solution may be a new piece of Apple gear or a problem solved by one of the Apple Geniuses or pictures taken on a guided Photo Walk.

(L) **Listen** for and resolve any issues or concerns – And when all else fails, Apple has developed a guide for its sales associates called "Emergency First Aid for Emotional Customers" that is heavy on feeling and empathy, such as "Listen and limit responses to simple reassurances," and "Acknowledge the customer's underlying reaction."

(E) **End** with a fond farewell and an invitation to return – As important as customers' first impression is, so also is the feeling that they have when they leave the store. So Apple trains on both the hellos and goodbyes to have customers take away good feelings, good memories and look forward to their return.

Christopher Ramey, of retail advisory firm Retail Rescue says, "Most luxury hotels train their employees every day, but my experience with retailers is they train every year, if that often," Ramey said. "The disconnect is obvious."

Ramey further notes the importance of providing sales associates with scripts for customer interactions at the opening, closing and throughout the service process, just as Apple has done. "Communications are powerful and today there can be little latitude for the salesperson to be flexible with words."

While people tend to think of Apple as a product company, it thinks differently of itself. "We think of Apple Retail as Apple's largest product," Ahrendts said when the company introduced the new iPhone X in Apple Park.

Apple retail generates 28 percent of the company's $229.2 billion net sales, according to the 2017 annual report and its impact not only on sales and branding but in personal customer connection are only going to grow.

Retailers that have yet to figure out the new retail business model for the experience economy, and most still don't have a clue, need to look to Apple for inspiration. Instead of "apple for teacher," it is Apple IS teacher.

Place Becomes Everyplace

The concept of Everyplace includes the idea of allowing customers to engage with brands on their own terms, through their own paths to purchase, whether it be online, in store, at home, or by phone.

Take the customer experience directly to the customer, face-to-face, person-to-person.

Many luxury brands have given into this idea of Everyplace by selling their goods online, but they've done it kicking and screaming, rather than embracing the opportunity to make their Everyplace meaningful and memorable.

And it doesn't have to be only via the internet, with its many different platforms (mobile, tablet, computer) to support. It can be taking the customer experience directly to the customer, face-to-face, person-to-person.

For example, custom-menswear brand **J. Hilburn** employs over 3,000 stylists across the country to meet with the customer to do personal fittings and give fashion advice in order to help select the right style and fabrication to suit the man and his lifestyle.

Or **Lincoln Motor Cars**, which offers its clients pick-up-and-delivery service whenever their cars need warrenty repairs. And this is offered across all its brands and through every Lincoln dealer. It is all part of "The Lincoln Way" of delivering services and experiences to its customers; in other words, Lincoln has evolved into the 4Es way of marketing.

CASE STUDY: Target

How Target is reimagining its Place

Coinciding with the news that Target is closing 12 underperforming stores comes the opening of its first "next generation" store design in the Houston suburb of Richmond.

Target's CEO Brian Cornell tantalized a recent ShopTalk audience with a preview of what was coming. "With our next generation of store design, we're investing to take the Target shopping experience to the next level by offering more elevated product presentations and a number of time-savings features," he announced.

What was promised at ShopTalk has now been delivered. The new 124,000 square-foot store at Aliana Market Center evokes a modern "Tarjay" aesthetic with large windows, polished concrete floors, natural wood accents and specialty lights. In addition to the enhanced style elements, the next-gen Target store has been realigned away from a strict racetrack format to include more engaging, circular department displays, as well as a circular central display area where special merchandise is featured.

Target's new look in its store is noteworthy, but what will be the big win for Target is its focus on building time-saving features into the next-gen store, specifically its two entrances that allow the customers to choose the way they want to interact with the store. Go in one door and the shopper can engage with the full-on Target shopping experience across the complete range of departments. Go in the other door and the shopper can pick up just what they are looking for fast and efficiently.

It's a mashup of convenience store and department store in one. On the convenience-store side, Target will feature groceries, including grab-and-go selections, wine and beer and other immediate needs, as well as a pickup counter for Buy-Online-Pickup-In-Store purchases. Dedicated parking spaces next to the convenience entrance will also facilitate BOPIS pickups delivered right to the car.

The devoted quick-stop parking spaces and separate entrance will immediately remove an obstacle to Target's grocery business. Now they just have to deliver with staffed checkout lanes, which the *Houston Chronicle* reported were in short supply when it covered the store opening.

In daring to reimagine a shopping experience that marries fast and browse-and-discover slow shopping, and the convenience of online with personal retail, Target will be rewarded. It has plans to extend the concept out to about half of its 1,834 stores nationwide, after the results of the Richmond live market test are read, as well as to open 100 small-format stores over the next three years.

Cornell has reason for optimism, as he shared with Associated Press, "We've been working all year to bring our new brand offerings to life, to bring more value to our guests. We have done a lot of work to reimagine stores and move into new neighborhoods."

If we've learned anything about today's shoppers, it is that they want it, when they want it, where they want it and how they want it as easily and efficiently as possible – online, in-store or increasingly a combination of both (BOPIS).

Traditional retailing strategies that require customers to conform to the retailers' set patterns don't work. The lines are blurred, as a recent survey conducted by Morning Consult among nearly 2,000 American adults, shows. When asked how they tend to shop most often, about one-fourth said online, 41 percent said in-store and 27 percent said they split it about equally between in-store and online.

This is the news that Target heard, loud and clear,

and has answered it with a new multi-dimensional store designed for the many different ways the guest, as Target calls the customer, wants to engage from one moment to the next.

Price Is Exchange

Retail thought-leader Robin Lewis has bemoaned the race to the bottom caused by retailers' reliance on price as driver for engagement. Without doubt, price still matters, even among the affluent with discretion to spend. But for the highest potential customers, the absolute price takes a back seat to value, as they are perfectly willing, and able, to pay when real value is there.

Exchange is the entire value experience a customer derives through the process of engaging with the brand.

Exchange involves more than money in the till; it is the entire value experience a customer derives through the process of engaging with the brand. Part of the exchange can be respect for the customer's time, which is at a real premium among the affluent. It can be special insider knowledge or know-how that helps customers navigate their lives. MAC cosmetics masterfully delivers expertise through makeup lessons and professional application.

Or a pay-it-forward gift of something meaningful that

is passed along, as **Toms** gives a pair of shoes to children in need for every pair of shoes bought, **Warby Parker**'s 'buy-a-pair/give-a-pair' eyeglass offer, or FEED bags which gives meals to the hungry for each bag sold.

Or it can be as simple as a meaningful thank you that makes the customer feel appreciated. **Beekman 1802**, the goats-milk soap company founded by the Beekman Boys Brent Ridge and Josh Kilmer-Purcell, that now has expanded into a full line of farm-to-skin beauty products, greets its Facebook followers every morning with a beautiful picture, often several of the Beekman farm. It's a personal way of saying thank you to their "neighbors," what the company calls its customers. Engagement becomes a no-brainer.

CASE STUDY: Revtown

Revtown offers luxury denim at affordable prices

In an already crowded jeans market, how can Revtown break through? That was my question to founder and CEO Henry Stafford when I learned about his Pittsburgh-based startup Revtown. His answer was simple, "We all wear jeans and everybody buys jeans. All of us in this company have been wearing jeans every single day to work for years, but we didn't love the product. If we could make jeans people actually loved, then people would buy our jeans."

Stafford says he grew up in the jean business, having originally launched his career in denim at American Eagle

Outfitters, then moving on to Under Armour for six years. In founding Revtown he is joined by other Under Armour alums, including Steve Battista, former senior vice president of creative with the company, and Matt Maasdam, the former head of the company's e-commerce unit.

Together the team defined the challenge, "How do we take the experience that we had building athletic apparel and put that same mentality into designing an amazing pair of jeans?"

The need: Jeans people want to wear at home

In researching the market, they found people aged 20 to 40 were wearing jeans five out of seven days a week, but the problem was as soon as they got home, they were taking their jeans off and pulling on something more comfortable. Men were changing into training pants or athletic shorts and women into yoga pants.

"We set a challenge to our design team to make a high quality, premium-designed jean that had to be comfortable and mobile enough to rival anything in the athletic world. That took over a year," Stafford says.

The key to the design process, they discovered, was the jean's fabrication and they had to go to a mill outside Milan, Italy to find it. "It all comes down to fabric and material development. We came up with Decade Denim fabric on which to build our jeans," Stafford explains.

"Our fabric offers great mobility, great comfort, and it's also woven with the strongest fibers that are used in apparel today, so it is incredibly durable. The fabrication is our innovation. There is nothing like it out there in the denim industry," he continues.

The opportunity: Premium look at an affordable price

With the right fabric in hand, for which Stafford adds they pay a premium price, they turned to a factory in Guatemala. "Our jeans are cut, sewn and washed by our manufacturing partner who's made over 150 million pairs of jeans. They make great product there and they do incredible washes. They are enabling us to scale quickly which is critical to our lean-operating, speed-to-market model," Stafford says, adding that manufacturing in this hemisphere was critical in the decision.

The efficiencies achieved through their business model allows Revtown to price its premium jeans at a flat $75 per pair, which means they can compete with mass-brands like Levi's and Gap on one end and premium brands found in department stores and specialty boutiques on the other.

In the jeans market today, Stafford sees the opportunity for Revtown to use a fast-fashion approach but to deliver high-quality product with it. "There is too much product out there where people are getting gouged because the model is so inefficient that the prices are way too high. We wanted to break through so the team shares that passion to create something innovative, creative, and efficient," he says.

Revtown's business model, which Stafford says is

another important innovation in the denim industry, makes that $75 price point possible. "Most every denim company out there does about 90 percent of their revenue on 10 percent of the SKUs. The remainder of the SKUs are inefficiency," he explains.

"For us it's very simple; we just focus on the top 10 percent. We offer the best colors, the best washes. We don't have inventory sitting in dead stores or warehouses. When we have demand, we cut, sew, wash the product and that ultimately allows us to keep lean inventories, react to consumer demand and to be in size and stock very quickly," he continues.

Taking Revtown jeans to market

Under Revtown's lean-and-mean business model, which comes naturally to co-founder Maasdam, who served 14 years as a Navy SEAL, the company will launch with a men's jean line in two basic styles, Sharp for a more refined look and Automatic for "any guy, any time, any place," the company describes. Filling out the men's line will be a selection of four casual Pima cotton shirt styles. A women's product line with the same DNA will be offered next year.

Revtown launched direct-to-consumer via e-commerce in keeping with its speed-to-market model. "It's no secret that e-commerce is growing far greater than any other channel of distribution out there and it will continue to grow," Stafford says.

"We look at consumer products and consumer

experiences as two different things. I believe people will leave their home to go to an experience. But they want products delivered to them at home. They want to touch and feel that product for the first time at home and reduce the friction of having to get into the car and go to the mall. The bedroom is the new dressing room," he says.

Revtown also has an answer to the subscription model that is becoming so ubiquitous in fashion e-commerce today, called the Crate. Rather than signing up for a regular shipment of new products, the customer can order a new wardrobe, once and done.

The bedroom is the new dressing room.

"We will give you the convenience to update your wardrobe immediately. Pick four things and we will throw in the fifth shirt on us, and in three clicks you have a new wardrobe: a couple of pairs of jeans and three shirts. We think it's a great way for people to update their wardrobe quickly and refresh things. And it is also incredible gift giving," Stafford explains, and adds at $230 the price of a Crate is less than one would pay for a pair of designer jeans at a department store.

"We think that's an amazing ridiculous price for the consumer and we are happy to provide that. In our lean-operating model, it enables us to be efficient so we can put all that money back into the consumer's pocket," he shares.

Revtown's story

In concluding our discussion, Stafford explains that being based in Pittsburgh, a Rust Belt town being invigorated by new industries, is an important part of the company's story. "Among this group, we all grew up in Rust Belt towns. It's part of the fabric of America. And we see denim as the iconic American fabric," he says.

So in naming the company – Revtown – three words kept coming up in their plans for the business:

- *Revitalizing* the jeans market with a new business model,
- *Revolutionizing* the way someone buys jeans, and
- *Reveling*, or celebrating why they are in business.

"'Town' is because we are really proud of the towns that we're from and what that means," Stafford continues.

"Pittsburgh is a hard-working town. It's an innovative town. So that's where we came up with the name 'Revtown,'" he concludes adding, "This is a fun business. We get to make product and market it and sell it. And that's fun and we revel in the fact that we can do that."

Promotion Is Now Evangelism

By making the brand experience meaningful and the exchange valuable, brands can tap the potential of its customers to evangelize the brand.

While luxury brands are wedded to the idea of traditional paid advertising and celebrity endorsements, creating individual brand evangelists that will spread the word about the brand is the highest mark of engagement and the ultimate in the new expression of marketing promotion. It's activated through content marketing, social media, traditional public relations, influencer blog posts, and through good, old-fashioned word-of-mouth marketing.

Brands must tap the potential of its customers to evangelize the brand.

That WOM is profoundly effective goes without question. In survey after survey of B2C and B2B companies, word-of-mouth is ranked among the most important marketing strategies. The Word of Mouth Marketing Association puts numbers on its impact: WOM drives 13 percent of sales, two-thirds of which is offline talking and sharing and only one-third social media driven. But for success, it takes a planning and organizational commitment, not leaving it up to chance.

Apple is one of the most effective brands in turning its customers into Evangelists. Outdoor brand **Patagonia** cemented its engagement with its brand loyalists in its "Don't Buy This Jacket" advertisement that encouraged its customers to think responsibly before buying new products. It underscored the brand's core value of quality and lifelong performance. It was such a remarkable program, it succeeded in positive buzz with a lot of people talking.

Beekman 1802's daily exchange of life on the farm pictures invites their neighbors into Josh and Brent's lives. It is a great example of brand evangelism designed to pull people in, rather than promotions that push out strong-armed marketing messages. Because the pictures are so remarkably beautiful, Beekman neighbors want to pass these inspiring photos along to their neighbors. Brent and Josh reject the 'lifestyle brand' label, in favor of being a "living brand." And so the story of the Beekman 1802 brand is spread.

CASE STUDY: Massdrop

Massdrop let's its enthusiasts spread the word

Most of us pay little attention to the keyboard that comes standard equipment with the computers we buy. Most computer companies don't either, says Will Bright, who heads up collaborations at **Massdrop**, an e-commerce company that organizes communities of product category enthusiasts and supplies products that meet their demanding wants and needs.

"There isn't a lot of innovation in keyboards coming from the companies. Yet it is the main tool people use to do their work on a computer, but companies throw the cheapest $20 keyboard into the box and call it done," Bright says.

But for some, keyboards are more than just an input

device. They are a passion. Massdrop has engaged over one million people who care deeply about keyboards. They spend countless hours thinking about, reading about, writing about and reviewing keyboards. And some even design keyboards, the best of which Bright and his Massdrop team guide through manufacturing and development to sell on the Massdrop site.

Take for example the Scrabble Mechanical Keyboard, designed by Cassidy Williams, a Massdrop community member, who incorporated the familiar Scrabble tiles onto a keyboard which offers users the tactile feel of a classic typewriter when keys are pressed, a feature that many enthusiasts demand. Massdrop collaborated with the designer to get the keyboard made and brought Hasbro on board to officially license the design.

The Scrabble Mechanical Keyboard was released just in time for National Scrabble Day, celebrated every year on April 13 to commemorate the birthday of Scrabble inventor Alfred Mosher Butts, born on that day in 1899.

Mechanical Keyboards is one of about 20 different enthusiast communities that Massdrop organizes, being its second largest community after audiophiles. It also has enthusiast tracks for men's fashion, beauty/cosmetics, DIY tech, auto, outdoor, cooking, quilting, knitting, writing, and watches.

How Massdrop got its start

Massdrop was launched in 2012 to organize group buys for enthusiasts of products from their favorite brands to cut out the middleman and get favorable group prices. Before Massdrop these types of group buys were organized from the ground up and conducted on an ad hoc basis.

Problem was these informal group buys were hard to manage and often times people were left in the lurch without products ever being delivered. Massdrop decided to organize these group buys in a professional way and build a business out of it.

To attract enthusiasts to Massdrop, it created forums where people could share their passion. And to facilitate those group buys, it created polls where customers could vote on the products they wanted. But that was just the company's starting point.

Massdrop's ultimate goal was to collaborate with companies to design products around the specifications and needs of its enthusiast audience. "From the outset of Massdrop, the big goal was to be able to not just take products that people want to do group buys for and make them available in a professional way," says Bright,"but to improve the products based upon what these enthusiasts are saying."

Bright explains that the enthusiasts use these products all the time and have thought about their usefulness and features far more than any product designer has or could. "If you are a product designer working for a company, you can only afford to think about that product for the amount of time your boss will let you," he says.

While enthusiasts may not have the right vocabulary

or skills to design products, they are the first to know when such products fall down or need improvement. "Enthusiasts know better than anyone how a product can be improved or made better. That was our goal: to take these kind of enthusiast insights to make better products for enthusiasts and ultimately better things for all customers," Bright shares.

At first when Massdrop approached a prominent headphone company about features that its audiophile community wanted, the company was skeptical. They weren't aware of the passion embedded in the audiophile enthusiast community and thought that their in-house designers knew better about what the customers wanted. Egos were ruffled.

But when Massdrop showed them that there were thousands of people online that care enough about the company's products to spend their weekends talking about them, they were willing to give Massdrop's community-based collaboration a shot. The result was 2,700 headphones were sold in just one week. Both Massdrop and the headphone company were convinced that collaborating with enthusiasts was a viable business opportunity.

Product enthusiasts are the Holy Grail of marketing

Today with over five million enthusiasts in a wide range of product verticals, Massdrop has been scaling its collaboration concept into new vertical communities, including audiophile, mechanical keyboards, everyday carry (tools, blades, flashlights), outdoor/Ultralight and men's fashion which is broken down into three sub-categories of heritage wear, formal wear and streetwear/techwear. These collaborations are marketed under the Massdrop Made brand.

Some collaborations come from product designers in the respective community, as with the Scrabble Mechanical Keyboard. In such a case, Massdrop takes designs from its community, manages manufacturing and distribution, and pays royalties to the community designer. For example, one young engineering student paid for college from royalties he made on a keycap design he created and sold on the platform.

Building a community of brand loyalists is the Holy Grail of marketing.

In other cases Massdrop goes directly to companies with community-generated ideas or increasingly companies come to them to tap the insights and innovations arising from the enthusiast base. So far it has worked with more than a dozen companies including Harman and Sennheiser for audiophiles and Allen Edmonds in men's shoes.

What companies get from these collaborations is far more than just another channel of distribution for products, but access to innovation sparked by enthusiasts – or in marketing parlance a product's heavy user – who know better than anyone what the products should be.

With unmatched loyalty and engagement, these customers are the Holy Grail marketers are searching for. "Once people start buying from us, they don't stop," Bright says, as he goes on to describe the demographics of the Massdrop community as primarily male, about 25 years of age, college educated and making $130,000 a year. On average the typical customer buys multiple items on Massdrop per year and with its expansion into beauty, knitting and quilting communities, more women are joining every day.

Massdrop is a truly unique business model

When I asked Bright about his competition, he said there really is no other company like it. Rather he says, "Massdrop is a mashup of Kickstarter and Costco – Kickstarter because we sell things before they are made and Costco because of the high volumes and low prices we can get." Even he is surprised by the passion Massdrop customers have for their particular category, being willing to put up hundreds of dollars in advance for products that won't be delivered for six to eight months.

What the Massdrop community gets besides the product at the end is a reward from being involved in the development of great product they care deeply about. They become co-creators truly invested in the product and its success.

"These people care to become part of the story," Bright says. "Our users keep coming back to see and engage in more discussion on the site."

The product enthusiasts that Massdrop has cultivated and nurtured have enabled the company to grow solely by word-of-mouth, with friends telling friends about things that excite them and are interesting to them.

Everyone in marketing talks about the power of user-generated content, but Massdrop has discovered the even greater power of user-generated products.

Answer Marketing's Higher Calling

The time is now to answer to marketing's higher calling by evolving from the 4Ps to the 4Es approach. It takes more than just a shift in tactics; it requires a complete reset of how you look at your customers and the ways you engage them.

Essential to the process is to talk with customers in a personal way and engage them in discussions about how they view your brand and ways they want to participate with it. This is the raw 'material' from which real insights can lead to innovation.

Help for Marketers

Today's affluent HENRY customer is looking for a more understated expression of style, not the arm candy that ultra-expensive bags represent, for example. They crave luxury in a brand new style. Rather than conspicuous consumption and status symbols that proclaim one's wealth, the HENRYs embrace brands that give them bragging rights to how smart and conscientious as shoppers they are.

For example, this past season's 'It' coat embraced by the wealthy wasn't one from a tony Madison Avenue furrier, but the **Uniqlo** Ultra-Lite Down Jacket which sold for less than $70. This jacket is cool and chic in an anti-status, conscientious-consumption, smart-shopper way.

CASE STUDY: Zara and H&M

In Fast Fashion, Zara wins with 4Es and H&M loses with 4Ps

Fast fashion is the darling of the fashion retail today. Whereas women's clothing store sales have declined 2.7 percent from 2016-2017 in the U.S., a recent report from Hitwise shows the fast fashion market has grown 21 percent worldwide over the past three years.

Two brands are the leaders in the fast fashion market: **H&M** and **Zara**, an Inditex brand. Given that both are international brands, it's hard to draw line-by-line comparisons for the U.S. market. But here is what you need to know. Zara is growing twice as fast a H&M, up 8 percent as compared with 4 percent from 2016–2017. H&M operates 536 stores in the U.S., while Zara operates about 300 stores here out of some 800 Inditex brand stores in the Americas.

FIT Assistant Professor of Technology Shelley E. Kohan and I shared our perspectives on the two brands and why Zara is doing so much better than H&M while operating in the same basic segment.

Our conclusion: H&M hasn't evolved beyond the 4Ps model of marketing – Product, Price, Promotion & Placement – while Zara is operating under the 4Es model in line with the expectations, wants and needs of today's customers.

H&M hasn't evolved from the 4Ps, while Zara has adopted the 4Es model of marketing.

For Zara, Experiences have replaced Product; Exchange is its Price; Evangelism is how it Promotes, and Everyplace is where it's at.

H&M still thinks product is king; Zara knows it's experience

In the new retail economy, experience matters more than product in the mind of the shopper. H&M has an overabundance of product to worry about, including a reported stockpile of $4.3 billion of unexciting, uninspired, unsold inventory. All that unsold product clogging up the stores needs tending. They are a mess.

Zara, by contrast, understands that customers want to experience shopping, not just buy products. Zara is an excellent purveyor of product, but it also capitalizes on the store experience by continuously offering reasons for customers to visit the stores and catch the hottest trends at affordable prices. Zara has created a loyal customer whose visit frequency is about six times per year, as compared to other retailers in the contemporary fashion market of two or three times per year.

The fast-fashion formula for success combines frictionless, expeditious shopping in a highly curated product environment offering scarce supply and new styles that rotate rapidly. The more quickly and efficiently a customer can navigate through the store to explore and find hidden gems, the better the experience. Zara nails that, while H&M requires shoppers to work to find what they want.

H&M focuses on price; Zara on exchange for value

The old pricing formula, "Pile it high, sell it cheap!" worked well through the 20th century, but in the new experience economy, it has been replaced by the concept of exchange.

Exchanging dollars for product is no longer meeting the needs of today's shopper as they strive for deeper connections with the brand. Retailers must adapt to the changing consumer where the top characteristic is VALUE=Time, Money, and Convenience.

Value is, of course, in the eye of the beholder. H&M's solution to its overstock problem is so old-school; a chain-wide fire sale is planned to rid it of its excess inventory. But with cheap prices being one of its primary appeals for customers, how much lower can it afford to go to keep its "good fashion at a reasonable price" brand positioning intact?

Zara, on the other hand, has a deeper understanding of the entire value proposition it exchanges with the customers. Today, value is measured beyond price, but also in time and convenience. In Zara's case, the fast-fashion deliverable is available in the quantity, format and time in which the customer needs the product. Zara expedites shopping for those in "great need" of time thereby creating great value, all the while exposing shoppers to an environment that allows for high engagement. That translates into great value.

Brand value aligns customer's needs with a brand deliverable. For example, the top loyal customers for retailers typically account for 80 percent of sales. These brand loyalists are also less price sensitive so strategies around tit-for-tat pricing, like H&M's, will never win.

Appealing to the loyal segment of the target market, like Zara does, allows for higher profit margins and caters to customers who seek out branded value.

Zara masters the art of branded value for their customers as they are not the cheapest in the fast-fashion arena but they consistently deliver branded value of trend-right product at affordable prices. H&M still thinks in terms of product-price.

H&M pushes its promotions; Zara evangelizes

By making the brand experience meaningful and the exchange valuable, brands can tap the potential of its customers to evangelize the brand. It requires brands to create individual brand evangelists that will spread the word. It is the highest mark of engagement and the ultimate influence in the new expression of pull, rather than push marketing. It's activated through content marketing, social media, traditional public relations, influencer blog posts, and through good, old-fashioned word-of-mouth marketing.

H&M is wedded to the idea of traditional paid advertising and push marketing strategies centered around capsule collections by outside designers. Today these strategies have become tired and formulaic. Its most recent collection by UK-based **Erdem** was a dud, despite being a designer brand favored by Kate Middleton, the Duchess of Cambridge.

Zara pulls its customers in and cultivates them as brand influencers.

Further, H&M recently found itself in a hornet's nest of bad publicity and social media outrage when it featured a young black boy modeling a sweatshirt emblazoned with "Coolest Monkey in the Jungle." In less than 24 hours it had over 18,000 retweets and 23,000 likes, or rather dislikes, as people were incensed by the insensitivity of the brand. Negative social media spreads like wild fire and can be the death of a brand.

Rather than push marketing out, Zara pulls its customers in and cultivates them as brand influencers to improve operations, services and products. They become brand evangelists who share excitement about the brand with their networks. Shopper frequency at Zara is two to three times higher than traditional women's apparel, which indicates super loyalty to the brand. Active utilization of social media by the customer base further drives loyalty and a connection to the brand.

Zara has a highly evolved data infrastructure that allows for super-efficient analysis of what's selling in the stores and what's being said on social media platforms. This data is used to improve various aspects of the business from product offerings to service enhancements. The two-way communication between the customer and Zara allows for continual improvement of product and services.

H&M thinks place; Zara is everyplace

Personal commerce is every place where the customers are, rather than only in the place the brand is physically present. This is the new distribution model for retailers today: Delivering the brand experience and products when and where the customer demands.

H&M has been slow to migrate sales online and sees a fix for the company in expanding its online presence. But that will fix only a small part of its problems. Its real-estate strategies, at least in the U.S., have been uninspired and heavily weighted toward malls where over 80 percent of its stores are located. With more than 500 U.S. stores, H&M faces off with all the other mall-based fashion retailers finding it increasingly difficult to gain traction in an already crowded market.

Zara, by contrast, is way ahead in its everyplace

strategies. It has devoted significant time, money and resources to synchronize online and offline commerce strategies. Linking a customer's shopping visit and providing access to inventory not present in the specific location allows shoppers to be in charge of their chosen destinations. It enables mobile connectivity as the conduit across various commerce channels and its mobile payment systems ease transactions on the customer's own terms. It is a big win for both the customer and the store staff.

And Zara's precise location strategy is another aspect of its everyplace factor. It currently operates in 2,213 stores across 93 markets and 39 online markets. The flagship locations are located in the most critical markets that appeal to their most loyal shoppers. Zara has the courage to continually strengthen its portfolio of stores by closing unprofitable ones, opening new markets, and expanding sister brands in existing markets (Zara Home, Massimo Dutti).

It's not about the brand (H&M), but about the customer (Zara)

Under the old 4Ps school of marketing, everything focuses on the company and the brand – its Product, its Price, its Promotion, its Place. In the new 4Es approach to marketing, it is all about the customer – Experiences for the customer, Exchange with the customer, Evangelism through the customer, and being Every Place for the customer. In essence, the customer becomes the brand manager.

It's the unique advantage that Zara has over its competitors, chief of which is H&M. Zara actually listens and reacts to customer feedback as its most valuable brand asset to improve its products and services. In 2016, the service agents responded to more than 17 million customer inquiries. Zara's foundational principal of focusing on people with initiatives on diversity, respect, equal opportunity, work-life balance and professional development further fosters a highly engaged workforce that translates into highly engaged interactions with customers. Additionally, over 60 percent of the Inditex workforce is age 30 or younger, aligning with the target market of the brand.

The result is the customer and the company work cooperatively together with the result that the Zara customer becomes the Chief Customer Officer.

In other words, Zara includes the customer in the decision-making process, whereas H&M dictates the decisions down to the customer, as in the old days when designers dictated fashion trends for the customer. But now the consumer calls the shots. Zara gets it, but H&M still has to learn it.

How to Be a Brand HENRYs Will Love

Tell New Stories of Luxury

For young HENRYs, who will become the next generation of luxury consumers, the goal of making more money, getting promoted, or becoming a partner is all well and good, but the traditional accomplishments are not the only prize they are after. Rather, it's the accomplishment of achieving a personal goal and digging deep to succeed at something truly remarkable, like completing an Ironman triathlon or doctoral dissertation.

These smart, accomplished young people know that just about anybody can make a lot of money, if that is what one aims for. But HENRYs measure their success in ways more personally meaningful than just financial success. That's why for many HENRYs luxury-brand watches have lost much of their status symbol cachet, since owning one mainly communicates financial status, i.e., how much money one makes and spends. Rather, HENRYs are looking for brands that communicate something more meaningful than just their net worth.

For young HENRY affluents, there is a distinct generational component to their chosen status symbols. They reject their parents' or grandparents' status symbols, in favor of symbols that communicate to their peers which 'tribe' they belong.

So HENRYs' status symbols are less about traditional high-end luxury brands and more about brands that really express one's values and identity. Think a **Mini Cooper**, rather than a **Mercedes**; or a **Filson** messenger bag, rather than one by **Louis Vuitton**; or a **Shinola** Runwell watch, instead of a **Rolex**.

Getting to the "why" of the brand is where the future of the luxury market will be built.

That said, the **TAG Heuer** watch brand, after an unsuccessful attempt by corporate parent LVMH to move the brand upmarket to compete in the luxury price range of $5,000 to $10,000, has recently reversed course, and brought the core of the product line back to a more affordable $1,000 to $5,000 with new positioning aimed at the spirit and mindset of the HENRYs.

Even at $2,000, a TAG Heuer watch is still quite luxurious, but the new branding tagline, "Don't Crack Under Pressure," and its alignment with youth-skewing celebrity icons, like Super Bowl champ Tom Brady, super-model Cara Delevingne, and tennis star Maria Sharapova, are intended to resonate with HENRYs. TAG Heuer also recognizes that today's HENRY women, as well as men, appreciate the high-performance promise that is a foundation of the brand.

Communicating a new style of luxury

In looking to the brand's future, it has just introduced the Connected smartwatch to compete with **Apple**, priced at a very competitive $1,500, designed and built with Intel and Google under the Android Wear operating system. Yet at the same time, TAG hasn't abandoned its legendary past and continues to offer its classic Steve McQueen line, in honor of a man who having never grown old, remains an icon for young HENRYs.

In a recent talk at the *Hackers on the Runway* conference in Paris organized by TheFamily, marketer extraordinaire Seth Godin asked "Is Digital the End of Luxury Brands?" Rather, the question should be "Is the Digital Generation, i.e., young HENRYs, the End of Luxury Brands?"

The key challenge for luxury brands with the young HENRYs is not about how they connect – internet marketing tactics – but how to create new and compelling reasons why their brands are meaningful and important to this digitally-empowered generation.

Getting to the "why" of the brand is where the future of the luxury market will be built. New branding strategies are what's needed, not just creative programming or digital-marketing tactics. It is all about tailoring the brand message to the unique psychology of younger consumers on the road to affluence.

Today, luxury brands telling stories of exclusivity, status, indulgence and over-the-top extravagance repel more than they attract. New narratives are required that maintain the elevation of the brand above the masses, yet connect with the unique consumer psychology of the next-generation luxury customer, which is democratic, not elitist.

Those new luxury stories that will resonate with the zeitgeist of today's young HENRYs and the next luxury generation include many thematic narratives. Here are some of the new stories of luxury that will connect with HENRYs:

Luxury of Performance

Luxury can't just exist as a product concept anymore, it has to deliver an experience that is meaningful to young HENRYs. It has to perform.

Brands for HENRYs must do more than simply 'be,' they have to 'do,' as Charles Revson reminds us when he explains that he makes cosmetics in the factory but sells hope to the customer in the store.

Brands have to deliver some meaningful, measurable value to the HENRY customer. Performance and function is a key differentiator. Performance takes brands out of the realm of simply being to actually doing something important for the customer.

Performance luxury is exemplified by brands like **Canada Goose**, a brand that has been around more than 50 years as the 'performance' brand for lumber jacks and polar adventurers.

Brands have to deliver meaningful, measurable value to HENRYs.

But Canada Goose shed its macho image on the cover of *Sports Illustrated* with supermodel Kate Upton wearing little more than a $595 Chilliwack Bomber jacket on a ship in Antarctic waters.

CASE STUDY: Canada Goose

Why Canada Goose will continue to be the proverbial goose that lays golden eggs

From humble beginnings in 1957 supplying down-filled coats and heavy-duty parkas to the hale and hearty working-class folks of our neighbor to the north, Canada Goose has rapidly scaled the social heights to become the "It Jacket" for Hollywood celebrities and super models at Sundance Film Festival and anywhere else the glitterati need to stay warm.

The brand is hot not because of the celebritics that wear it, but the fact that it does its job really well – that is keeping people warm when it gets extraordinarily cold. In doing so, the Canada Goose brand has become the proverbial goose that lays golden eggs.

Canada Goose is on a tear

Since 2015, the company's revenues have grown 77 percent, from C$291 million to C$591 million in fiscal 2018. In the past year alone, it boasts 46.4 percent revenue growth, with direct-to-consumer sales more than doubling year-over-year (121.3 percent).

DTC now accounts for over 40 percent of total sales generated from stores located in premier shopping destinations in seven cities (London, Toronto, New York, Boston, Calgary, Chicago and Tokyo) and its website now serves 12 countries. It further distributes products wholesale in 2,200 points of distribution across 38 countries.

In reporting the company's banner year on June 15, 2018, it also announced plans to open three new stores in North America ahead of the 2018 holiday shopping season, in Short Hills, New Jersey; Montreal, Quebec; and Vancouver, British Columbia. This follows news in May that the company would open flagship stores in Beijing and Hong Kong and will expand e-commerce in China through a partnership with Alibaba Group.

Commenting on the company's stellar performance, Dani Reiss, president and CEO, said, "These results reinforce my belief that we are still just scratching the surface of our global potential. As we continue to bring more

Canada Goose to more of the world, we are resolutely focused on the long term and what we need to get there."

Credit Suisse agrees that Canada Goose is just beginning, in a research note published in March 2018. It reported Canada Goose holds approximately a 6 percent share of the $11 billion premium outerwear market and is rapidly gaining on **Moncler**, its primary competitor with 16 percent share. "GOOS has substantial untapped global opportunity," the report stated. "We forecast a +23 percent revenue CAGR in '18-'20 – an incredibly scarce growth algorithm vs. global apparel peers." By 2020 the company plans to operate 20 stores globally.

Global expansion is a priority for Canada Goose, which describes itself as a "three-season lifestyle brand." In so doing, it has expanded its product offerings from extreme winter clothing to lighter weight choices for spring and fall. With this broader product range, its jackets are suited to consumers in places where winter may be more like a Canadian spring or fall. It also is extending into knitwear and accessories so that Canada Goose brand can be a choice to wear under those parkas too.

Canada Goose's time is now because it hasn't abandoned its working-class roots in search of the allure of the luxury market. Rather it is translating its rock-solid form and function for a new class of consumers who need it, want it and will pay for it, without the extravagant excesses that traditional luxury brands charge their customers.

Canada Goose delivers superb value in new luxury style for today's conscientious, social justice, values-focused HENRY consumers.

In with "New Luxury," Out with the Old

Canada Goose has accomplished so much in such a short time and is poised to continue to attract more "Goose People" – what it calls its customers – because it captivates today's affluent consumers who crave luxury in a brand new style.

The problem for heritage luxury brands, like Moncler, is that the positive values that luxury brands have traditionally filled – quality, style, workmanship, design – are increasingly being satisfied by premium and lower-priced brands, or challenger brands as consulting firm Deloitte describes them in a study of what makes millennials spend more.

"The great challenge for brand owners seeking to capture the affections of millennials is how to communicate to a generation with shifting preferences and loose brand loyalties, and for whom no single channel appears to be significant," the report states, noting that challenger brands have a leg up on traditional luxury brands fixed in their old luxury ways. Canada Goose is one such challenger luxury brand, with prices for its jackets ranging from about $500 to $1,500, a premium price, but well below Moncler which retail for about $1,000 to $2,500+.

Luxury that does more than just look good

Canada Goose avoids the pitfalls in the negative

connotations associated with traditional luxury by playing up the positive attributes of luxury in quality, workmanship and design with a practical, performance edge. If Canada Goose can keep researchers in Antarctica warm, it can keep young, urban professionals in Boston, New York and Chicago warm too.

Being a performance brand, Canada Goose is made relevant to HENRYs.

In being a performance brand, rather than just a luxury brand, Canada Goose is made relevant to young consumers who need that top-of-the-line performance, not just some showy luxury label. Canada Goose is a practical choice for affluent consumers with a capital P. It sloughs off the elitism implicit in traditional luxury brands like its coats shed ice and snow.

Luxury with a conscience

Being a sustainable and ethical luxury brand is high on the list of expectations for young American affluents especially, with Deloitte finding that 48.9 percent of U.S. millennials surveyed always consider a brand's ethical stance before purchasing. This compares with 31 percent across its sample of 1,000+ millennials including those in the U.K., China and Italy. While they don't buy simply because of these ethical concerns, it gets a brand like Canada Goose into their consideration set when it also checks other boxes on their priority list.

Recently Canada Goose has taken some heat from People for the Ethical Treatment of Animals (PETA) in its sourcing of coyote fur for its jackets. In response the company has instituted a traceability policy for fur and down used in its products, "to ensure they are sourced from animals that have not been subjected to any unfair practices, willful mistreatment or undue harm, and materials are fully traceable throughout the supply chain," the company states.

The company is also committed to other environmental and social issues, specifically to save polar bears through support of Polar Bears International. To that end it produces a custom line of PBI products donating a portion of sales to the cause, with all items accented with a Pantone custom color called "PBI Blue." To date the company reports donating $2 million to PBI.

And for native Northern Canadians, the company donates fabrics and materials through a Canada Goose Resource Centre program that provides Inuit sewists with modern materials they can use in their traditional ways of sewing.

Authentic luxury for authentic people

With a goal to build brand awareness, it is using an integrated marketing approach by telling the authentic story of Canada Goose and its Goose People through film and books. The idea is to make impressions, not buy them.

In film, Canada Goose products are used both in front of and behind the camera, being worn on screen in *Manchester By The Sea* and *X-Men 2* for example. But more importantly, Canada Goose is the choice of film crews making movies in cold climes.

It also is an official sponsor of a number of film festivals around the world, especially those focused on independent filmmakers. "It's our way of celebrating the hard work of those who have experienced the unparalleled functionality and warmth of our products," the company states.

Perhaps the most compelling stories about the authenticity of the Canada Goose brand come from its Goose People. Rather than hiring spokespeople or brand ambassadors, it understands its authentic Goose People tell the story best, including arctic explorer Ben Saunders who was the first person to complete unsupported ski trips to both North and South Poles and Marilyn Hofman, a medivac flight nurse, who was saved by the buoyancy and warmth of her Snow Mantra jacket when she fell through the ice on the Churchill River.

Since publishing its first Goose People book in 2007, Canada Goose has continued to tell its Goose People stories online.

Canada Goose is new luxury for a new age

HENRYs want luxury that is more inclusive, rather than exclusive. Canada Goose may be premium priced, but it is accessible to those who really need it.

They crave luxury that is authentic and made for them, not some celebrity. Canada Goose has kept its hard working roots for every man or woman that needs to stay warm in Antarctica, the slopes of Mt. Everest or the streets of London, New York, Montreal, or Chicago.

Create-Your-Own Luxury

While Boomers were once known as the "Me-Generation," young HENRYs have taken it to a whole new level. They are a generation raised on self-expression about everything, including their own skin, which has become a canvas for personal expression and creativity in the form of tattoos. The emotional drive for self-expression in home furnishings that adapt to all different room sizes and life stages is what **Lovesac**'s Sactionals furniture concept provides.

Millennials are a generation raised on self-expression.

Lovesac is a brand better known for its iconic beanbag chair. Today, Lovesac offers a uniquely customizable and innovative take on conventional upholstered furniture. Its Sactionals are described as a cross between "upholstery and Legos™." Sactionals consist of two basic upholstered pieces that can be combined in any configuration imaginable – no tools necessary – to create customized seating configurations from a compact loveseat for a studio apartment to a conversational arrangement to fill a super-sized great room.

With a starting price over $2,000 for a basic loveseat configuration, Sactionals can be pricey for many young couples starting out, but the add-on flexibility that allows the furniture to grow and change as the couple's needs change is the ultimate in luxury. Sactional furniture expresses an upscale performance vibe that delivers a personal experience in both design and function.

Lovesac's success marketing to young HENRYs is undeniable. It was named to *Furniture Today*'s list of the fastest growing furniture retailers, posting a gain of 33.9 percent from 2016 to 2017 to reach $101.8 million in sales. That puts it at number 67 in *Furniture Today*'s Top 100 Furniture Retailer's List for 2018.

Make it personal

There are many ways marketers can personalize their offers to HENRYs:

- **Personalized Product:** Offer unique product with a wow factor that meets personal needs of HENRY customers. Curate product selection to tell a personal story about your brand that connects with the most valuable, high-potential customers.

- **Personalized Service:** Understand that the people that sell your brand, from the stock room, customer service manager to the selling floor all must work together with one focus: Delighting customers with an experience customized to their special needs and desires.

- **Personal Customer Connection:** Build a loyalty bond with HENRY customers using social media and internet tools and techniques.

CASE STUDY: Interior Define

Interior Define sells custom design at affordable prices in ways HENRYs like to shop

Showrooms, light on inventory but heavy on customer experiences, are a rapidly growing model in retail. And not just for digitally-native brands that want to cross over from the virtual world to the real one, but also for real-world retailers that need to add an additional experiential component to their mix, like the **Nordstrom Local** concept store that just opened in Los Angeles.

It has no inventory but serves as a guideshop to help customers select fashion online, as well as offering custom tailoring and beauty services along with drinks to enhance their Nordstrom experience.

Digitally-native home furnishings brand, **Interior Define**, is on the forefront of the showroom trend. It is crossing over into the real world with its customized furniture shopping experience in two new showrooms in Austin, Texas, and Los Angeles. "That means there will be a location in the brand's top four markets: Chicago #1, New York #2, Los Angeles/San Francisco #3 and Austin #4," says Rob Royer, the company founder and CEO.

Interior Define became Royer's personal mission after being dissatisfied while shopping for furniture to decorate his home. This experience occurred shortly after he joined omni-channel retailer Bonobos as Director of Customer Relationship Management. Finding a lack of high quality design and meaningful customization at an affordable price in the furniture offered at retail, Royer decided he could do it better.

Born on the internet, Interior Define is now growing in the real world.

Interior Define was born in 2014 using the internet to allow shoppers to fully customize their furniture design online with each piece made to order. That strategy eliminated investment in inventory in order to offer attainable price points.

Early adopters among the millennial and Gen X HENRY customers that Interior Define targets signed on. Nonetheless, Royer faced a challenge to reach a wider swath of customers who were unwilling to spend thousands of dollars on a sofa or chair they haven't seen or sat on in person, despite the company's 365-day return policy. So I/D Guideshops were born, starting first with the company's Lincoln Park, Chicago home base, then NYC's SoHo location in May 2017.

Powered by technology, delivered personally

Royer is using his CRM training to match his understanding of I/D's existing customer base to map locations where the brand can reach like-minded customers with similar furniture buying needs. "We selected markets largely based on where we had developed a concentrated online customer base," Royer explains. "We seek locations where our core customers, both demographically and psychographically identified, are well represented." But then an additional filter is added, says Royer, "We want to open in close proximity to relevant, digitally-native lifestyle brands."

Its Austin location filled with young HENRYs drawn to its many cutting-edge employers, checks all the boxes. "Beyond the incredible growth and vibe of the city, I/D's core customer is well represented: savvy, design-conscious consumers who understand one size (or look) doesn't fit all," Royer says.

Plus it is located in the vibrant Domain NORTHSIDE lifestyle village. "Domain NORTHSIDE in Austin has done an impressive job of curating relevant lifestyle brands. It gives us the opportunity to coincide with other digitally-native vertical brands like Warby Parker and Bonobos, as in our Chicago and SoHo locations. But unlike our first two markets, Austin will also position I/D among furniture comps like CB2 and Restoration Hardware," Royer notes.

With the Austin region being a hub of technology companies, the Interior Define Guideshop is bringing an enhanced high-tech feature to its high-touch experience. As in its other Guideshops, the Austin store has large touchscreens where customers can view any design (in any of its 70-plus colors and numerous configurations) that match their personal style and interior aesthetic.

Then in Austin it is adding a 3D product configurator enhancement giving customers the ability to view their I/D sofa, chair and bed selections in rooms decorated with non-I/D products including rugs, lighting, and accent table styles. "While Austin is a brand new location, we've applied our learnings from our Chicago and Soho Guideshops to inform how we designed the space utilizing new technology, all within an efficient 1,800 square feet," Royer says.

Maintaining synergy between Interior Define's internet-first profile and its physical person-to-person connection is critical to the brand's success, Royer says. "From the earliest days of our first Guideshop location in Chicago, we witnessed the power of marrying a unique, physical presence with our online experience."

"Our Guideshops locations enable customers to test the product in person and to ask questions face-to-face (with the same team members who serve our online customers). Our design associates walk customers through our brand story and product options in a friendly, low-pressure environment." Royer continues. "We've seen brand awareness increase faster in our Guideshop markets and ultimately boost online sales, which continues to represent the majority of our business."

The key to success in the showroom retail model is to seamlessly blend the internet and showroom experience. "Similar to the approach we've taken to our web experience, we look at our Guideshops as an opportunity to completely rethink the concept of furniture retailing – making it a more unique and comfortable experience. Inside our Guideshops, we've designed our physical brand experience as an extension of our web experience. In addition to an assortment of our core designs, we display the extensive customization options available, as well as digital displays that help customers visualize options not merchandised in the spaces," he continues.

For the future, Royer and the Interior Define team will continue to look to establish footprints in authentic neighborhoods with a new-age vibe and where its data suggests there are customers with a real-world need for its internet-powered made-to-order furniture. "We will extend our retail presence in 2018, both through innovative pop-up experiences (similar to the experience we recently launched with Batch in San Francisco's Russian Hill neighborhood), as well as additional long-term Guideshop locations," Royer concludes.

Luxury of Convenience

Subscription-based marketing seems like the latest and greatest new business-building idea. With exciting startups showing the way, including companies like **Ipsy** and **Birchbox** in beauty, **Blue Apron** and **HelloFresh** in meals, **Dollar Shave Club** and **Harry's** for men's shaving products and **Stitch Fix** and **Trunk Club** in fashion, subscription-based marketing appears to be the ticket to grow a business with a loyal consumer base that can be counted on for a steady stream of repeat business. It is reported that **Under Armour**, **Target**, **Walmart**, and **Sephora** are testing the concept.

By anticipating customers' needs and meeting them in advance, subscription programs offer a meaningful luxury to HENRYs who are busy navigating their lives.

Prospects in subscription marketing look bright, with a new study by McKinsey & Company reporting that subscription e-commerce has grown by over 100 percent a year over the past five years, to reach more than $2.6 billion in sales in 2016.

Subscription programs offer a meaningful luxury to HENRYs who are busy navigating their lives.

Such a rapid pace of growth makes sense considering that so many new players are piling on, in categories as diverse as beer and wine, child and baby, meal kits, pet foods, vitamins, fashion and underwear, and replenishment services for basics like contact lenses, cosmetics, men's shaving, and women's feminine products.

Subscription marketing is hot, but you can get burned

But before jumping in with both feet, the McKinsey study reveals the painful realities of subscription marketing. Based upon a survey among more than 5,000

U.S. consumers, it finds only 15 percent of online shoppers have taken the plunge into the subscription lifestyle for consumer goods. Online streaming services, however, have a much higher participation rate (46 percent).

While awareness of subscription offerings is fairly high at 53 percent, actually converting those aware of subscription plans is still low, with 13 percent saying they've subscribed at one time and only 8 percent currently subscribing. In terms of subscribers, the replenishment-style of subscription plans (e.g., Dollar Shave Club, Amazon Subscribe & Save) have higher rates of conversion, than do curation-style programs (e.g., Birchbox, Blue Apron, and Stitch Fix).

As hard as it is to get new customers, it is even harder to keep them. The McKinsey survey found that nearly 40 percent of subscribers cancel out of their subscriptions, with one-third canceling after only three months and over half only sticking around for six months. In particular, meal-kit programs have the highest fall-off rate, with 60 to 70 percent of subscribers pulling the plug after six months.

These stats reveal the dark underside of subscription marketing. And that reality hasn't changed since e-commerce-fueled marketing has replaced the old direct-mail continuity and club plans of the past, explains Georg Richter, a 30-year veteran in subscription marketing.

"My whole career has been in subscription. I've done Book-of-the-Month Club, Doubleday Books, Columbia House Records, Scholastic. I've been CEO or president of these companies," Richter shares. "That led me to **Guthy Renker**, one of the premier direct marketing companies that have subscriptions at its core."

Two years ago Guthy Renker spun off a separate company called **OceanX** with Richter as CEO. His job, and the new company's mission, is to guide companies into the brave new world of subscription marketing. "We help other companies get into the subscription channel. We have 12 clients right now and many more in the works with large CPG companies and retailers. It is a very hot business these days," he says.

New world of subscription marketing

From his perspective as a leader in the subscription industry's shift from the old model to the new, I asked Richter how things have changed. Aren't these new plans just like the old book-of-the-month club programs disguised in sheep's clothing?

"No, it's very different," he explains. "In the old world you had hard relationships, heavy late fees, and it was difficult to cancel. We used crazy promotional offers to get people in and had to be hard on the backend to make sure people stayed with the program so we could make money. It was a transactional business."

Today, he says, the subscription programs must have a much softer relationship with customers. It depends on the marketer understanding each and every customer and meeting their individual needs. "A subscription can't be a burden. It must be a great experience," Richter says.

What hasn't changed from the old to the new subscription model is the cost of acquisition. He relates that about one-third of revenue must be set aside for new customer acquisition and that it represents the single biggest category of spending. "You constantly have to acquire new customers. It's just part of the model," he says.

The biggest change in customer acquisition has come about by the rapidly expanding channels through which they are acquired. Where it used to be limited to three or so channels, such as direct mail, inserts, TV and some radio, today it requires managing at least 20 channels on various platforms including Facebook and Twitter, each with their own nuances of customer behavior demanding distinctive offers.

Watch and learn

Looking across the subscription ecosystem with new subscription programs popping up in many different segments, I asked Richter if there was a first-mover advantage, where the first company into a segment grabs the best prospects.

He says no, the first in may well be the first out. "Being the first mover is not an advantage at all. Think about Birchbox. They were the first into beauty sampling, but now Ipsy is much more successful. Or Dollar Shave Club. They were sold to Unilever, but they are not as successful as **Harry's** now."

Companies that wait behind the first movers and learn from their mistakes have the advantage of doing it better.

But, Richter advises, those followers need to do something different or better and offer a new twist to the leader's offering.

Create forever members

Another thing that hasn't changed from the old to new subscription model is churn. Richter says the key is to think beyond the transaction to create a relationship that goes deeper. "We have to work toward forever memberships," he says. "We have to think about why they quit, then add elements to the program that give them more reasons to stay on than to get out."

For example, every subscription package needs to include something interesting and even more engaging than the last shipment, in order to inspire and surprise the customer. Subscription packages must also include a cliff-hanger that makes them hungry to get the next delivery.

"It's about inspiration, not a transaction. It's about storytelling and feeding that customer relationship. These things will result in people staying for a long time," Richter shares.

Get timing right

He goes on to advise on a critical factor unique to subscription programs: Cadence or the schedule in which new packages arrive. Each subscription program has different demands that make for the optimum cadence.

For example, for a shaving club, where a new blade is needed weekly, a monthly delivery of four razors is the right cadence. Such a cadence might be too frequent for fashion packages, which will do better on a bi-monthly or quarterly schedule.

Curate selections

The value of subscription services, ultimately, comes down to the ability of the plan to curate the experience including the product selection to the specific needs and interests of the customer.

"There is too much product out there. It's the paradox of choice," he says. A subscription plan can be a convenient way for customers to discover wonderful things that make their lives more interesting, more fun, and more fulfilling.

In conclusion, Richter believes there are opportunities in almost every consumer goods category, though he is cautious about meal-kits since they are costly to implement properly and too many things can go wrong from preparing and packaging of the kits to setting the meal on the table.

He sees **Albertsons** with its recent acquisition of **Plated** better positioned for success in that arena thanks to having prep kitchens in its many grocery stores.

"Subscriptions today are about relationships, not transactions," Richter concludes. "This is a type of marketing that puts the person at its core – true one-on-one marketing. Too many manufacturers, CPG companies and retailers think about the product and its specs, not about the person. With subscription plans, the customer has a deeper relationship than just buying more stuff. They want to become part of something special and to belong."

Subscriptions today are about relationships, not transactions.

The key to success in subscription plan marketing is to build a relationship of trust with the customer and that requires understanding the underlying psychology of consumers.

CASE STUDY: Gap

Gap subscriptions for busy HENRY parents

Subscription programs are rapidly emerging as big brand's new obsession. These programs are seen as the way to respond to customer's demands for more personalization, customer service and relevance in a retail market overcrowded with choices.

By hooking onto consumers' on-going need for replenishment in consumable categories, like beauty, personal care, food, beverage, household supplies, or updates to customers' wardrobes or simply the novelty of receiving something new and different on a regular basis (curation-style programs), brands hope to create demand through a new method of delivery when their traditional means, in-store or online purchase, are losing traction.

That seems to be the guiding light for Gap's launch

into subscription marketing aimed at HENRY mothers for their children's fashion needs. Moms can start with babyGap's OutfitBox for curated and coordinated selections of baby clothes every three months that are sized up as kids grow at $70 for $100 worth of clothes or BedtimeBox at $49 for three pajama selections worth $75. Then they can graduate to **Old Navy**'s Superbox of kiddie clothes for ages 5 to 12 for $70, reduced from $100, with a $10 discount on the next delivery if no items are returned from the previous box.

In the category of kids clothing, Gap is going head-to-head with **Kidbox**, an investment-backed startup which offers 6 to 8 selections for $98 and **Rockets of Awesome**, which ships an 8-piece mini-wardrobe seasonally with prices ranging from $16–$38 each (average price point is $18.75). But whereas Kidbox sells a mix of well-known labels, like Adidas, DKNY, 7 for All Mankind, Puma, Jessica Simpson, Reebok and Diesel, the babyGap and Old Navy plans offer only babyGap and Old Navy styles, which may get stale after a couple of seasons.

"Marketers must rise head and shoulders against the competition to gain and keep market share," says Jim Fosina, CEO of Fosina Marketing Group, an online marketing company specializing in subscription plans. "This is a branding and marketing requirement which is completely channel agnostic."

One of the biggest gaps in Gap's subscription plans remains: Will customers want to dress their kids like models in a babyGap or Old Navy advertisement every day?

Can the Gap offer the customers enough variety and selection to keep them in the program season after season?

Subscriptions must provide a real service

That Gap is providing a potentially valuable service to customers is without question. They don't have to go to the store or sit at a screen to scan options and make purchases. The Gap does it for them. "No doubt, moms of young children will see this service as a tremendous help in taking care of their children," Fosina affirms.

But he warns that Gap's success in this new approach hinges on "the ability of the retailer to think and act like a very smart direct marketer," which it hasn't been traditionally.

"It is important that Gap understand their subscription-service-customer's profile in real-time and allow the subscriber to adjust a set of variables in the box prior to shipping. There is nothing worse than missing the mark in terms of what customers like and prefer," he adds.

How will Gap integrate subscriptions with stores?

As a boots-on-the-ground retailer, Gap has the potential of developing relationships with its customers that could be further enhanced with the added at-home service of subscription delivery. That being so, its stores seem to be one of the best ways to get people into their box programs and beat the digitally-native kids clothing programs like Kidbox and Rockets of Awesome.

The question then becomes how will Gap integrate

subscription marketing into its stores or even online, as a visit to the Old Navy website doesn't offer a link to the Superbox program on the home page.

Will in-store personnel be trained to upsell customers at the counter into the subscription program? And is Gap ready, willing and able to be channel agnostic in its subscription aspirations or will it keep subscription operations siloed as a separate unit? Further, will Gap be able to integrate data about in-store or customers' online selections into upcoming subscription boxes?

Gap's success in subscriptions hinges on its ability to create deep and lasting relationships with customers.

"Gap has to keep quality, responsiveness to the mom's preferences and 'likes' and price/value relationship front and center in all engagements with their customer," Fosina advises, which clearly includes both their subscription-originating preferences and their in-store and online selections too.

Ultimately Gap's success in subscriptions hinges on its ability to create deep and lasting relations with customers. "Gap has to build a familial relationship with 'Gap Moms' so that the experience is equivalent to having a personalized shopping partner that understands the child or children in making selections in the boxes," Fosina says. "This service like many others will be competing with the ability for moms with small kids to purchase a wider assortment of clothing through other channels more cost effectively."

So far, Gap sees promise in its initial subscription efforts. "As the subscription box scales, there are some changes in the numbers, but overall we're seeing low returns, high retention and we're bringing in a number of new customers to Gap through the model," a Gap spokeswoman told Digital Commerce 360.

Collectible Luxury

Tapping into an individual's collecting instincts is the ultimate way to build brand loyalty. One brand that has exploited the collecting passion of consumers is **ALEX AND ANI**.

ALEX AND ANI may be best known for its series of expandable wire bangle bracelets, each with a small charm attached. Not only can these bracelets (and the companion necklaces and earrings) be adjusted to each wearer, they are made for collecting.

The bracelets are ideal for today's "stacking" trend, such that a wearer can choose multiple bracelets, each with a charm and beading that is significant to the person, with designs for both him and her. Sample charms include a variety of shapes and symbolic icons that encompass spiritual, religious, travel, and hobby themes, as well as licensed themes including sports-team logos, sorority letters, and others.

Each bracelet is highly affordable, starting around $30, meaning the wearer can buy one for pocket change. But the concept is aimed at collecting, so a woman's stacked collection adorning her arm can total several thousands of dollars, bought in $28 increments. The collectability of ALEX AND ANI is a hook that guarantees a continued flow of sales for the brand.

The idea of create-your-own jewelry is not new. Many customers still love the customizable bracelets from **Pandora**. But ALEX AND ANI have taken this concept a step further by offering a product that is virtually limitless in its expansion possibilities.

While Pandora-style bracelets are restricted to the circumference of the wearer's wrist, the ALEX AND ANI bracelets are designed to be laddered up the wearer's arms, as many or as few as he or she likes – for ALEX AND ANI, unlike Pandora, offers designs for men.

The formula is working for ALEX AND ANI. The company has experienced meteoric growth, with sales skyrocketing from $5 million in 2010 to over $500 million in 2016, insiders say, with a net profit margin, according to private equity database Pitchbook, that was recently 23 percent. The company's success has propelled company founder and CEO Carolyn Rafaelian to the number 18 spot on the 2017 Forbes list of America's Richest Self-Made Women – owning 80 percent of a company worth at least $1.2 billion.

Its jewelry boasts made-in-America credentials and is crafted from environmentally sustainable materials. The company claims its products are infused with "positive energy," so these items incorporate the element of experience that has been so successful for luxury brands. ALEX AND ANI bracelets turn a memorable experience into a concrete and fashionable, jewelry statement piece instantly.

CASE STUDY: 1stdibs

1stdibs is designers' best friend, now it wants to be consumers'

1stdibs is an international online purveyor of antiques and one-of-a-kind furniture, decorative accessories and collectible objects d'art. Originally launched to serve the needs of designers for unique, collectible items for the lifestyles of the rich and famous, now it is looking more broadly to satisfying the collecting passion of a broader consumer market – the HENRYs.

"The race for the $50 online business is already won by Amazon. But the race for $5,000 is still on. 1stdibs wants to win that one," says David Rosenblatt, CEO of 1stdibs. They are well on their way with an average order size of $3,000 – a price point that many HENRYs can trade up to when their collecting passion is tempted.

If you are unfamiliar with 1stdibs, don't blame yourself. Rosenblatt didn't know the company either when he was first approached by private equity group Benchmark to take the reins after it made a sizable investment in the company.

"The first person I called was my own interior designer who I was in the middle of a project with and asked him about it. He said, 'Half your apartment is from this company.' So I was immediately interested," he told me.

1stdibs then

1stdibs started life in 2001 and overnight became interior designers' best friend. Founder Michael Bruno got his inspiration browsing the Paris Flea Market, the world's largest, where the finest European antiques and 20th-century design is found. He saw the opportunity to bring those resources to the rest of the world through an online marketplace.

So Bruno partnered with some Paris dealers and built a website to list their products. Interior designers immediately came on board, as they realized they didn't have to travel to Paris to shop for their customers. More dealers in the U.S. and throughout Europe followed and a thriving under-the-radar business was born serving interior designers and cognoscenti seeking distinctive one-of-a-kind objects to decorate their homes.

Rosenblatt joined 1stdibs in 2012 after selling the online advertising company DoubleClick to Google where he served as president of display advertising for a year. With his internet advertising credentials, he was a prime candidate for 1stdibs, which at the time was largely an advertising platform for its dealer/partners who paid a monthly fee in exchange for the right to list items. "We were like Craigslist," he says.

That changed as Rosenblatt led the move from an advertising medium to a full e-commerce marketplace. "Our mission is to create a global marketplace for the best design in the world," he explains. "Today that means e-commerce. It's the way people want to buy. It works across all time zones and allows us to create lots of advantages for our buyers and sellers that don't exist in an advertising model."

1stdibs now

One of the values that 1stdibs gives its buyers and sellers is assurance of authenticity and provenance in the things it sells, unlike **eBay**. "Only authorized dealers can list items, no individuals. And in order to list, a dealer or brand needs to pass a comprehensive application in the vetting process. We are highly curated on the supply side," he describes.

In order to stay on 1stdibs, dealers must also maintain a high service record, as they handle fulfillment of orders and pay 1stdibs a commission on sales. He adds that the company has more sellers from outside the U.S., primarily Europe than they do inside the U.S.

Today 1stdibs has over 500,000 products listed from several thousand dealers worldwide who serve buyers in more than 50 countries. Originally servicing primarily the interior design trade, 1stdibs claims 40,000 registered designers among its loyal followers. But where designers lead, in-the-know consumers follow.

Today designers represent only about 40 percent of

its business, with consumers making up the lion's share. "We have about five million visits to the site each month," Rosenblatt shares.

What draws these collecting-inspired consumers to 1stdibs is easy to understand. "We are a marketplace of one-of-a-kind luxury objects," he says, noting that besides furniture and decorative objects for the home, 1stdibs also offers art, jewelry, vintage fashion and now contemporary artisan design.

"Most people want authenticity in their lives, and most especially in their homes. Home is the expression of one's personality and interests. The objects in our marketplace are different than what everyone else has. Our customers don't want their homes to look like a page out of a catalog or be the same furnishings you can buy in a furniture store. All five million of our customers can buy something truly unique and different on 1stdibs," Rosenblatt continues.

To keep its edge, which Rosenblatt describes as a "competition of aesthetics," 1stdbibs has branched out to the artisans and craft makers into contemporary design. "We see the opportunity to help these artisans come to market in the same way we saw the need for dealers selling antiques and 20th-century objects 10 years ago. There is an explosion of interest in contemporary design among interior designers and consumers today."

As he grows the company, Rosenblatt takes a broader view of the role 1stdibs plays in the luxury goods market.

"One way we view 1stdibs is as a marketplace for luxury design," he says. "But we are on the cutting edge of the migration of luxury into the digital realm."

With a history that started with antiques, then into 20th-century design, and now contemporary design, art, jewelry and vintage fashion, 1stdibs spans a range of luxury consumers' interests. "We are a vehicle for the migration of the luxury market as a whole from offline to online."

In first joining 1stdibs, Rosenblatt was struck by the power and potential of its business model to satisfy the cravings of luxury-inspired consumers for unique objects that reflected their personal passion. "I saw the discrepancy between how important 1stdibs was to designers and the low profile it had in the consumer market in general. We are planning to change that," he says.

Value Luxury

A compelling luxury narrative for young HENRYs is value. These younger consumers are, as a rule, intent on maximizing their return on investment when it comes to the products and services they buy. They diligently research purchases, tapping into their social networks to find the right combination of quality, service, and price. They aren't afraid to pay a premium, if they find the right match.

For HENRYs, luxury is a state of mind, not a price

point or brand. And marketing is about creating perceptions and translating the context of luxury into something meaningful and important for HENRYs.

For HENRYs luxury is a state of mind, not a price point or a brand

Value is in the eye of the beholder and that means the customers' perception is critical for success. That is a lesson learned, and proven by mass-market priced Suave shampoo, a **Unilever** brand.

CASE STUDY: Suave

How Unilever's mass-market Suave brand proves luxury is a mindset

Fast Company reported that **Suave**, "fooled a bunch of beauty influencers into thinking it was luxury haircare." It changed its name to Evaus (Suave spelled backwards), redesigned the package, gave it a premium price and presented it to a group of beauty bloggers and influencers to test. The result: The influencers bought it!

The bait-and-switch test was done to challenge the common belief that "women are skeptical of quality if the price tag is too low," explained Jennifer Bremner, Suave's brand director. She cited brand research that found seven in 10 millennial-aged women believe that premium or high-priced brands are more "trustworthy than value or lower-priced brands and products."

To prove the point, the bait-and-switch idea behind Evaus was born. "On Suave, we learned from our listening that labels and price tags can play an outsized role in purchase decisions," Bremner said.

This is certainly not news to me. Packaging, positioning and price play a huge role in how consumers perceive products. The more premium-looking the packaging combined with convincing promises of enhanced quality and excellence in performance, the more elevated the brand in the customers' mind which then justifies paying a higher price. That's because . . .

In marketing, perception is reality

The Suave-Evaus test proves that by changing the customers' perception, marketers can change their business reality. If customers are persuaded that they will get a heightened, more luxurious experience, as the Suave experiment did, they are likely to get it. That is because luxury is a state of mind, not a brand or a price point.

How can marketers create that luxury perception? By telling new stories of luxury that are interesting, meaningful and relevant to the next generation of customers that mean growth now and in the future.

"Shoppers' most valuable asset isn't their dollars, it's their attention," says Christopher Brace, CEO at Syntegrate Consulting in New York. "Millennials are especially influencing this area because they don't buy things, they buy stories." It's a battle for the customers' minds, not their wallets, where the brand marketing wars are fought.

CASE STUDY: Wayfair

For Wayfair deep discounts are not enough

In April 2018, **Wayfair** offered a day of "amazing deals" on all that's home, right when more people are moving or on the lookout for fresh home decorating excitement. "Spring is the season when our customers are especially focused on sprucing up and furnishing outdoor spaces in anticipation of warm weather and summer entertaining," said Steve Oblak, Wayfair's chief merchandising officer, in announcing the 24-hour Way Day promotion.

In Way Day, Wayfair positioned its day as the new "retail holiday," joining **Amazon**'s Prime Day, to give customers a chance at enjoying deep Black-Friday discounts. And like Amazon's Prime Day, Wayfair offered flash sales for a limited time throughout the day, like a 4-piece sofa set with cushions for $282 and a Charbroil gas grill for $302.

The strategy was borrowed from Amazon's playbook, which was first launched in July 2015. But unlike Amazon Prime Day, which is only open to its Prime members, Wayfair's Way Day celebration was open to all.

And also unlike Amazon, which wasted no time announcing the results of its first Prime Day on July 16, the day after, Wayfair has remained mum about its results, other than a brief mention in the company's 1Q2018 report. "Most recently, we were excited to see the success of Way Day," the company stated, as it reported a sales increase of 47.7 percent year-over-year and a 33.2 percent increase in active customers in the first quarter ending March 31, about a month before Way Day.

This may tell us all we need to know about the first Way Day promotion. It wasn't the big deal that the company hoped for, otherwise it would be out beating its chest like Amazon did after its first Prime Day.

Way Day brought more traffic

We can get an outside-in look at the results of Way Day from big data compiled by SimilarWeb, a digital data analytics company. Its data shows that on Way Day, Wayfair's online traffic peaked at 2.7 million visits, which was 75 percent more than its 1.6 million daily average. But even when Wayfair increased traffic on its most popular day, it still received just 5 percent of Amazon's traffic on April 26, compared with 3 percent on any other day. SimilarWeb reports that Amazon averaged 59.3 million daily visits in the past year (May 2017–April 2018), compared with Wayfair's daily 1.6 million average.

Wayfair visitors also spent more time and clicked on more pages that day than is typical. On Way Day people spent an average of 9 minutes on the site and clicked on 10.2 pages each visit. This was an increase of over 3 minutes and 4 pages per visit though the rest of the month, SimilarWeb also reports.

The results show much greater levels of consumer engagement on Way Day compared to any other day for Wayfair, but 9 minutes to make a decision about buying a new sofa or bedroom set seems unrealistic. Since Wayfair's average order size was only $236 during the first quarter of 2018, it suggests the company is selling a whole lot more decorative accents than major furniture pieces. So 9 minutes may be more than adequate time to click off an area rug, lamp, set of pillows, or an end table. But a sofa? I don't think so.

On the plus side, Wayfair got on a lot more people's radar screens thanks to the Way Day promotion. Direct traffic from organic search rose from 284,000 visits on Tuesday before Way Day to 570,000 on Wednesday, April 25.

"Seeing traffic from direct visits double is incredibly valuable, as this source is the best indication of brand strength," says Ethan Chernofsky, director of corporate marketing at SimilarWeb. "Seeing the primary growth channel coming from one so closely associated with brand awareness is a huge sign that Way Day benefits will continue to be felt for a long time to come."

Be careful what you wish for

From the outside then, Way Day looks to have been a digital success, "helping the site increase traffic immensely," Chernofsky contends. However, as much as Wayfair has been growing revenues, $5.2 billion in the 12 months through March 31, 2018, it has been losing money even faster. In 1Q2018 its net loss rose 90.6 percent, to $107.7

million from $56.5 million in 1Q2017, nearly twice the rate of its sales increase of 47.7 percent, from $961 million to $1.4 billion.

That is the kicker: more customers and more sales means even more loss for the company. A recent analysis from professors Daniel McCarthy, Emory University, and Peter Fadar, University of Pennsylvania, found that Wayfair loses $10 on every new customer acquired. Wayfair pays $69 to get a new customer, but each one only yields a lifetime contribution to profits of $59.

More customers and sales for Wayfair mean more loss for the company.

This study was conducted to argue for new customer data metrics to value public companies, using Wayfair and **Overstock** as case studies, not because of any inherent interest in these companies, but simply that each provided public data needed for their analysis, specifically revenues coming from new customers and existing customers who are being retained. That both companies compete in similar home verticals also proved useful, since furniture is a category with long purchase cycles. However, the professors argue that their analysis model applies even for low frequency purchases, since a customer is a customer regardless of how often he or she buys.

Regarding Wayfair, Fadar said:

> They're spending like crazy to acquire very, very inefficiently. If you just look at the surface level, you see this kind of hockey stick, exponential growth. But it's all acquisition. They're just getting a bunch of people to come in. Those same people aren't coming back nearly as often as you might expect them to be. In fact, their repeat purchase rates are a lot lower than they were for Amazon, even close to 20 years ago. And this is from their own data."

Overstock, by contrast, does much better than Wayfair in their analysis, spending only $38 to acquire a new customer and generating $47 in profits afterwards. They concluded that customer retention needs to be where Wayfair should be investing its efforts, which is where Overstock, and Amazon for that matter through its Prime subscriptions, is focusing.

"While one could argue that some of Wayfair's advertising expenses are earmarked for customer retention, the proportion is likely to be small, and because Overstock is a relatively more mature business, its corresponding proportion [in customer retention] is likely larger than Wayfair's," Fader said.

At the end of the day, Way Day may have been a success in bringing lookers and buyers to the site. But Wayfair needs to figure out how to get the customers it acquires for a premium to buy more often and spend more when they do. Until it figures that out, there is no way forward for Wayfair. As a result, Way Day looks to have only added to the company's loss, rather than its profitable growth.

Luxury of Comfort

For HENRYs luxury must not only look good but feel good. It is experienced by the luxurious touch of hand and envelops the wearer in ultimate comfort and security, which is made meaningful by not threatening their lifestyle with budget-busting prices.

The **Splendid** clothing brand, sold in its own stores, online and through luxury retailers like **Neiman Marcus** and **Nordstrom**, makes softness and comfort its primary selling proposition. It provides substance to the style by explaining the difference, then delivering on that promise of comfort: It describes its brand of comfort as "soft, indulgent fabric, hugging you all day long."

Linen bedding company **Boll & Branch** makes luxury bedding comfort a key part of its unique selling proposition. Its stated mission, "To make better sheets by making a better Company. We choose to source the world's finest organic cotton, treat our workers well by having Fair Trade certify our supply chain. And, most importantly, we choose to sell our products at fair prices." But it also plays to other important luxury stories like value luxury.

Perhaps no place in the HENRYs life is comfort so important as in sleep. **Casper** has disrupted the traditional mattress business being the first online bed-in-a-box brand. It now is working on disrupting the traditional model for retail mattress shopping by making that uncomfortable shopping experience comfortable too.

CASE STUDY: Casper

Casper plans to sell more mattresses by getting people to sleep on it

Casper, the online bed-in-a-box pioneer that disrupted the traditional mattress retail business, is doing it again. This time, it is bringing the experience of sleeping in a Casper bed to a whole new level. Casper has opened its first nap showroom, as opposed to a bed store, in New York City, called The Dreamery. It is a place where people can actually sleep, rather than just buy a new mattress.

The concept is simple, and brilliant. People can schedule a nap break at The Dreamery to enjoy 45 minutes of rest in one of its nine Casper-equipped sleep pods fully decked out in Casper beds, sheets and pillows with a sleep mask included. After nap time, guests can enjoy a cup of coffee in the lounge. Bathrobes, ear plugs and makeup wipes are also available to make guests feel comfortable. Walk-ins are also welcome.

Luxury must not only look good, but it must feel good.

The Dreamery's 45-minute block is based on science that finds it is the optimum time people need to refresh and recharge in the day, without feeling groggy afterward.

A nap will cost $25, a small price to pay for improved health and productivity. "The Dreamery is about making sleep and rest a part of our regular wellness routines – similar to how many people prioritize a workout class," said COO Neil Parikh in a statement. "The concept enables us to pilot new ways of bringing better sleep to more people and to more places – whether that's here, the workplace, airports, or beyond."

From online to physical retail

The Dreamery takes Casper to a whole new level in experiential retail. Since its founding in 2014 as an exclusive e-commerce business, Casper has been expanding rapidly in physical retail, starting first in 2016 in partnership with West Elm, which ended after a year, coincidentally not long after it announced a new retail partner.

In May 2017, Casper joined with **Target** to put its mattresses and bedding products into 1,000 Target locations. For Target, Casper is more than just a bedding brand to stock in its stores. Target invested $75 million in the company, becoming the lead investor in a $170 million round of funding that was used to launch a design lab in San Francisco, as well as "to pursue other brick-and-mortar opportunities," the company stated.

Not long after, Casper opened 15 of its own branded pop-up shops in major cities across the country. A special feature in each pop-up shop is a home-like setting where customers can test drive the mattresses for 20-minute trial sessions.

But that was clearly not enough time to get the full Casper sleep experience. So when it opened its first permanent showroom in New York this year, it took retail space in the same block for The Dreamery.

Retail success by focusing on how you sell, not what you sell.

Casper disrupted the traditional business of mattress retail because it evolved from the 4Ps of marketing approach that is so evident in traditional mattress retail: Product, Price, Promotion and Place. Here's looking at you, Mattress Firm, blanketing the country with over 3,000 retail locations.

What Casper understands, and too many mattress retailers like Mattress Firm don't, is that they are not just in the business of selling mattress and bedding products. They are in the business of providing customers with a better sleep and shopping experience. The products they sell are only the means to that end.

Casper operates under a new 4Es model of marketing:

- **Experience** (better sleep and mattress shopping) replaces Product (new mattress);
- **Exchange** (What is the value of a better sleep and mattress shopping experience?) becomes the new Price (How much can you discount to get people to buy?);
- **Evangelism** (pull people in for a better sleep and mattress shopping experience) rather than Promotion

(push out paid advertising to promote sales); and

- **Every Place** (Casper is available everywhere people have a smart phone, tablet or computer) is new Place (mattress store).

Yes, Casper is in the business of selling more mattresses and bedding products. But it focuses on people's sleep problems and, even more importantly from a retail point of view, their mattress shopping problem. Casper solves those problems by not just selling a better mattress for less, but by remaining focused on the customers' complete experience.

Casper pulls customers in with an evolved 4Es of marketing approach. Casper understands that it is not what it sells, but how it sells it that will win customer loyalty, support and business.

Now all Casper has to do is scale it and to do that it will take its Dreamery concept into new, unexpected places where people have sleep problems, like airports, office parks, and busy city streets. The best marketing and the best branding will be when people think about sleep, they think about Casper. The Dreamery is one powerful way to do that.

Bespoke Luxury

HENRYs demand a true 'customer-centric' experience, not in words as many big brands do, but in reality, like today's innovative brands do by necessity and design.

This is why there is a bright future for bespoke footwear for young HENRYs as they grow in their careers. Unlike Boomers who wore $10 Keds or $25 Chucks in their youth, the Boomers' GenX and Millennial children grew up in $100 Air Jordans. As a result, their sneaker wardrobes, specially crafted for each and every kind of sport and athletic endeavor, were a major capital investment.

Young HENRYs are a perfect fit for bespoke shoe brands which offer hand-crafted shoes like **Berluti** and **Tod's**, both brands expanding to the U.S. They are also customers of disruptive brands like **handmadebrogues.com** which offer made-to-measure shoes at around $200 to $300. This is affordable luxury compared to the $675+ to step into a pair of custom-made Tod's Gommino Club driving shoes or $1,990+ Berluti Oxfords.

There are many ways marketers can personalize their offers to HENRYs:

- **Personalized Product:** Offer unique product with a wow factor that meet personal needs of HENRY customers. Curate product selection to tell a personal story about your brand that connects with the most valuable, high-potential customers.
- **Personalized Service:** Understand that the people that sell your brand, from the stock room and customer service managers, to the selling floor all must work together with one focus: Delighting the customer with an experience customized to their special needs and desires.

International fashion brand, **Suitsupply**, does both.

CASE STUDY: Suitsupply

How Suitsupply has HENRYs' needs covered today and tomorrow

Upwardly-mobile HENRYs – men with Suitsupply and women with Suistudio for women – are just the kind of customers that **Suitsupply** cultivates: highly-educated professionals who need to dress for success in their management, law, finance, and consulting careers, but who may not yet have a lot of cash to spend.

Since its founding in 2000 in Amsterdam, Suitsupply has been an unqualified success. Launched out of the trunk of Fokke De Jong's car, giving new meaning to "Trunk Show," Suitsupply has been helping men worldwide "find their perfect fit" in tailored fashion.

Starting first with an online direct-to-consumer model, Suitsupply carved out a niche in men's suiting and tailored fashion, which is defined by the essential element of a jacket. "We were an omni-channel retailer before they invented the term 'omnichannel,'" De Jong says. Today about 30 percent of company sales are conducted online.

Online shoppers are guided in the fit process with a Fit Finder app, but many men want more hand holding in selecting, sizing and styling their looks. That is where the Suitsupply stores come in. "Service is critical today. In our stores shoppers can interact with someone who is an expert in men's tailored fashion," he continues.

Now having spread across Europe, Asia, Australia and North America and closing in on 100 destination locations, including 31 stores in the United States and five more slated to open in 2018, and the rest of the globe online, Suitsupply is venturing into new territory – the challenging world of women's fashion with a new sister brand Suistudio.

Suitsupply sells high-quality, well-designed men's suits at affordable, even reasonable prices. Its off-the-rack suits start under $500, with made-to-measure up to $2,000.

Delight customers with an experience customized to their special needs and desires.

Despite rumors that the men's suit is dead on the altar of casualization, De Jong says the elevated elegance a tailored jacket gives to a pair of jeans, for example, fits the look that many men want to project. "I've been reading about death of the suit for the last 18 years," he quips. "It's not happening. For many brands a suit is pure conformity. It is stale. But we make it as an expression of individuality for a man, not conformity."

De Jong wants to bring that same approach to tailored women's fashion, which he believes is ready for an elevated fashion experience like Suitsupply delivers for men. Now with three stores, including a flagship in New York at Brookfield Place on Vesey Street and others in Shanghai and Amsterdam, Suistudio has the same basic corporate DNA as Suitsupply but with XX instead of XY chromosomes.

"Suistudio is based on the common denominators that set Suitsupply apart, which is luxury fit and tailoring at an attainable price point. But with women's fashion we bring new style energy into the environment," De Jong tells me. Suistudio will build on the same fundamentals that made Suitsupply a success. Those pillars of success are: vertical integration, word-of-mouth marketing and destination location shopping.

Vertical integration control of quality and price

Being a vertically-integrated company, Suitsupply and Suistudio have complete control of the quality of its garments, including the finest Italian fabrics, design, manufacture and distribution.

By exercising full control over the entire process, the company can offer luxury-quality fashion at "attainable prices," which in the case of men's suits translates into $2,000 tailored quality at a $500 price point. Women's fashion will reflect the same price advantage.

"No other company has carved out a business model and product segment that provides customers with the style, quality, personalization and great prices in the way that Suitsupply has," he continues.

Pull, not expensive push marketing

Because of its amazing quality and equally amazing prices, Suitsupply has been able to grow organically without significant investment in marketing and advertising. Social media and word-of-mouth marketing is its marketing weapon of choice.

"Our informed customers have spread the word about the brand and we create 'sticky collection campaigns' that keep the public talking," De Jong shares.

Instagram is one of its primary social media channels with over 400,000 followers enticed with the tagline line, "Don't just fit in, find your perfect fit."

Become a destination people will search out

With endorsements from Suitsupply's passionate customers, its word-of-mouth and digital-powered pull marketing strategies (as opposed to expensive paid push marketing) allows the company the luxury of making its stores true destinations that people are eager to search out.

"We create in-store shopping experiences that are memorable and emphasize the customer experience above all else. It's one of the core strengths of our business model," De Jong says.

"We create interesting stores with well-trained staff and have tailors on site. People find us to find their own perfect fit. We don't rely on the classic retail real estate traffic play." For example, its Chicago showroom on Rush Street is a two-story affair, featuring a penthouse garden terrace to enjoy drinks after or during shopping. Its Greenwich, CT store is in a remodeled historic mansion on a partly residential street.

The new women's Suistudio stores will emphasize

personalized service in an interesting store setting. Each Suistudio store will be a separate store, not co-located in a menswear Suitsupply store.

Personal fit first and foremost

For the Suistudio brand, De Jong sees providing women with expert tailoring to achieve a personal, custom fit may be its biggest opportunity. "Fit is even more important for women's fashion. It was harder to figure out, but I think we nailed it," he says.

Deliver a WOW factor that will hook customers and bring them back for more.

"The reactions we are getting now is it is a unique experience for women, because men have been used to being tailored in suits. Women have never been able to walk into a store where you have beautiful product for attainable price points but also where there are tailors in store and alternations being done on the site."

Bringing fit and fashion together in an upscale women's shopping environment is the big opportunity for Suistudio.

Suitsupply knows its customer – young, ambitious professionals and his or her needs today, but is positioned to meet those needs in the future, as these individuals advance in their professions with the ability to trade up.

It's the affordable front door to a bespoke fashion experience that today's young and less affluent HENRY customers will ultimately grow into.

Suitsupply looks to be a sustainable brand with a powerful target market - young men and women with ambition and incomes destined to rise year-over-year with a need for professional fashion and appreciation for high levels of service. The brand has ticked off all the most important boxes to succeed.

- **Identifying the customer:** Young professional HENRYs who need professional suiting.
- **Defining what he/she needs:** Fine quality suiting and women's "power dressing" at reasonable prices today with offerings that can grow with his or her ability to pay in the future.
- **Delivering a WOW factor that will hook customers and keep them coming back:** Service levels that exceed what they would expect and probably have never before experienced. By providing instant alterations, Suitsupply builds a level of trust and loyalty that will bring customers back again and again.

Luxury of Simplicity

Today, more than ever, the KISS principle – Keep It Simple Stupid! – is valued. Embrace the concept of simple things elevated.

In the world of food, what could be more humble and simple than grits, a Southern food staple. Celebrity chef, Vivian Howard featured on PBS' *A Chef's Life* about her Chef & the Farmer restaurant in Lenoir, North Carolina, dedicated a show to grits where she took the quintessentially Southern, and most basic of ingredients, into gourmet dishes acclaimed by chefs and critics. "Pimp my grits" is about taking a "humble ingredient and elevating it."

Simplicity is hard to do, but beautiful to behold.

Personal care and beauty brand **Kiehl's** sells simplicity itself – simple product, simple ingredients, simple packaging – and extraordinary results.

The label spells out its flagship Crème de Corps body lotion's point of difference with quality ingredients. The simple bottle announces the luxury is inside the bottle, not what's on the outside. It's prominent "since 1851" heritage says a brand that has been around that long must be doing it right. Kiehl's simplifies its packaging and presentation elegantly.

Simplicity is hard to do, but beautiful to behold when it is achieved. "Less is more" becomes the guide to creating simple, elegant brands and brand stories.

Simple elegance defies ostentation or extravagance. Simple elegance is communicated in all brand touch points – from promotion, to packaging, branding, and positioning.

Simple elegance pays attention to the minute details and shows how those details transform the product into an experience, like back-to-basics brand, Detroit Denim.

CASE STUDY: Detroit Denim

Detroit Denim taps maker culture

Incorporated in 2010, **Detroit Denim** produces "handmade selvedge jeans," from unwashed, 100 percent cotton, raw denim, the classic fabrication for jeans, but which has been largely abandoned by modern manufacturers.

Priced at $250 for men's and $200 for women's, Detroit Denim promises exceptionally long wear backed up by a lifetime guarantee for repairs, great fit suited to different body types and authentic detailing that pays homage to the jean tradition.

At its founding, owner Eric Yelsma planned only to sell the jeans wholesale, but decided to open the company's first store after discovering locals were interested in buying direct from the maker. Originally he set aside a portion of the workshop floor for retail, that it quickly outgrew.

Today the company has a new storefront which has become a place where Detroit Denim can tell its unique story, make a connection with customers and deliver a service experience unmatched at other jean retailers.

"I never intended to be a retailer. It was quite accidental," Yelsma said. "But people were hungry for the connection, to learn about who made their jeans, where they were made, how they were made. That is what the store provides."

While still small, making only 20 pairs of jeans per day and selling a narrow band of styles in its store and online, it is slated to produce 250 pairs/day in 2020 and 1,000 by 2023, which will mean more jobs for skilled craftsmen and women, more jobs at retail, and support for the company's digital presence.

Luxury in Wellness

CPG companies are faltering as they fail to meet consumers' growing demand for healthier foods. In the past year, Kraft Heinz, Campbell Soup, and Nestlé all cited demand for healthier options as hindering growth.

This is a sign of a greater trend in the consumer market, not just for healthier foods but for goods and services that promise a healthier lifestyle. An emerging rank of new companies are moving swiftly to fill the void and grabbing market share that the traditional companies have left open.

Wellness today is not just a trend or a fad; it's a way of life for more and more people. "Wellness is an approach to living life that is becoming as second nature as brushing teeth," says Kelsey Groome, managing director at TRAUB, the global development group, and author along with associate Katie Guiheen, of a new *Wellness Journey* report. "Brands that will have the biggest impact are ones that will make it accessible to more people to live a balanced life in mind, body and soul."

The report maps out eight major segments in the wellness market – fitness, meal programs, supplements and vitamins, eateries, juicing, spa, beauty, and meditation – and identifies 100+ companies that are trailblazing in each of those segments.

Rather than calling the Wellness 100+ disruptive brands, I see them as competitors more in tune with the evolving needs of today's consumers. Whereas traditional companies are struggling to adapt, these Wellness 100+ brands have grown out of an understanding that wellness is not the result of one or a range of products, but a lifestyle that needs a range of goods and services to support it.

"The 100+ brands on our wellness journey," they write, "are indicative of a broader lifestyle movement to prioritize wellness for physical, internal and spiritual health. The proliferation of these concepts is set to continue as wellness shifts from a singular goal to a lifestyle habit."

The market that these Wellness 100+ brands compete in represented a $3.7 trillion global wellness industry in 2015, according to data compiled by the Global Wellness Institute, which will release an updated report later in 2018. In 2015, industry growth was predicted to exceed 17 percent through 2020.

I asked Groome and Guiheen to give me a guided

tour along their wellness journey and call out the movers and shakers that are most relevant to retail. Here are the stops along our journey:

Build a product brand leading with services

The first movers in the wellness market have focused on physical health: fitness, beauty and spas. And many of these players combine health services in store with products to take home to support consumers' wellness lifestyle.

Retailer **Dry Bar** leads with premium blow-dry and styling services in 70+ salons plus it offers branded products in each shop, online and with partners including **Nordstrom**, **Bloomingdale's**, **Sephora** and **Ulta**, so customers can maintain their looks at home. And on its website, customers can view videos that give them professional blow-dry styling tips.

Heyday brings the same stripped down, simplified approach to beauty facials, offering a range of customized facial services including walk in or a monthly subscription plan. Heyday salons also offer a curated, multi-brand range of products for sale. Currently Heyday has 5 NYC locations, but it is a concept poised to grow nationally like Dry Bar.

Body beautiful

NYC–based fitness fashion retailer **Bandier** sells women's clothing, shoes and accessories so she can workout in style. And it also devotes space in its Flatiron location for her to attend workout classes in its Studio B. In so doing

Bandier combines fitness and fashion in one location.

Sporting equipment brand **Peloton** takes a different approach, leading with its premium fitness bikes to support customers' fitness at home, and enhanced with streaming fitness classes from its NYC studio so the exerciser can virtually join an expert-directed class without actually being there. With 30+ showrooms nationwide, Peloton also sells apparel and accessories to take the Peloton lifestyle further.

Essential nutrients, rather than supplements

The traditional approach to nutrition is that it is something added to or supplemented with, as opposed to the radical idea that people choose foods based upon the nutritional value that is already in them. This may contribute to CPG's missteps in the wellness market and **Vitamin World**'s failing.

"The new age of supplements and vitamins focuses on being all natural and in line with the transparency millennials are seeking," Groome says. "Understanding what is going on in their body is key, and vitamins and supplements that can do that with a personalized approach are gaining market share." She further points to studies that found 70 percent of millennials say they use herbal remedies and 68 percent have tried homeopathic cures.

Dirty Lemon Beverages is a brand taking an essential nutrient, rather than supplemental approach to consumers' health. It offers a range of drinks formulated to provide essential vitamins and nutrients targeting specific customers' needs, such as energy, beauty/radiance, anti-aging, vitality and detox.

Gender-specific health solutions are the anchor for two new healthy brands. For women **Ritual** simplifies the multi-vitamin formula by providing the essential vitamins most women lack. And all ingredients are open-sourced which adds to transparency. Groome also notes that Ritual has raised nearly $15.5m to date from high-quality investors (Forerunner, NVP, Founders Fund, etc.)

For him is **Hims** which takes a similar gender-specific approach to men's health issues with natural remedies for men's most pressing health concerns, hair loss and erectile dysfunction, plus male-centric skin care.

In vitamin supplements, custom packages of daily doses are rapidly replacing a shelf of bottles in mega-doses. **Care/of** fills that prescription with personalized daily vitamin packs based on a consumer's initial screening of lifestyle and goals. This is another company gaining takers not just among consumers but from venture capitalists too, having raised $15m Series A in July 2017 from RRE and Goodwater Capital, which value the company at $35m.

Go to the mall and get healthy

"People must have a reason to go to the mall, then they will shop, but shopping can't be the reason to go there," says Ken Nisch, chairman of retail design from JGA. That is the answer to the retail apocalypse laying waste to so many regional malls.

Fitness centers provide one of those reasons to go to the mall for the wellness minded. "Fitness and wellness concepts will increasingly act as important anchors to malls," says Groome, pointing to how well malls can meet demands for space, parking and other facilities that empty anchor-store shells can accommodate.

Brands must enter a new era with focus on sustainability, experience, minimalism and wellness.

Equinox clubs and fitness classes is one of the leaders in appealing to the next generation's fitness needs where and when they want them, like in Los Angeles' Westfield Century City mall where it is an anchor.

Equinox is also expanding into hospitality at the new NYC–Hudson Yards mall opening in 2019. Equinox Hotel Hudson Yards will include 60,000 square feet of indoor and outdoor club space and pools, as well as spa and hotel facilities.

Westfield Century City mall also hosts a wide variety of wellness-focused retail-cum-services tenants, including **Forward**, a new-age personalized doctor's office, **House of Polish** for healthy manicure/pedicure nail services, and a multitude of healthy-food options serving organic, vegan, gluten-free snacks, juices, and tonics, alongside more typical food court fare.

This is but a short list of the must-see stops on TRAUB's comprehensive wellness journey covering eight major wellness "destinations" and including 100+ wellness brands. "Our compilation of brands is illustrative of how expansive and increasingly accessible this space has become," Groome and Guiheen write.

In this report, they continue, "We identified the brands that are defining a new era of retail as well as the values that are behind those brands: sustainability, experience, minimalism and wellness. As we journey into 2018, we reflect on the rise of wellness concepts that consumers have embraced as part of a collective modern mantra of living a healthy and balanced life."

To which, I add, studying what these emerging wellness brands are doing to meet the needs of today's, not yesterday's customers might provide a valuable guide to retail's journey to wellness and health as well.

Luxury of Discovery

Thrill of discovery invites HENRYs to spread the word. Discovery anchors the most powerful marketing tool: word-of-mouth.

Brands can use the luxury of discover as vehicle to spread the word about the brand through customers (discoverers) own social media.

In his best-selling book, *The Purple Cow,* Seth Godin calls on brands to be not just good, not just reliable, but to be remarkable. That is what activates word-of-mouth and makes a brand grow. Questions are:

- What thrill does your brand deliver?
- What unexpected discovery is waiting for your customers?

Brands gain much more power through postings by customers on their own social media connections than any posting from the brand itself.

Take **Bare Minerals**'s powder foundation. Who knew ground up rocks could provide such good coverage and be so good for your skin? It was a revolutionary idea that had to be shared.

Or exclusive e-tailer **Project Gravitas**, which got started doing the one essential LBD (little black dress) customized 8 different ways for every woman's body type. The thrill of discovery gave women something to shout about and share with friends.

Or **Farfetch** that lets HENRYs discover fashion in boutiques world-wide.

CASE STUDY: Farfetch

Fashionistas Discover Fashion in Far-Flung Places

In luxury circles Farfetch, the digital fashion marketplace founded by José Neves that offers selections from nearly 900 fashion boutiques worldwide, is often compared to **Yoox Net-a-Porter**, the multi-brand online platform recently acquired by **Richemont** in a reported $2.7 billion deal. Now Farfetch is headed toward a U.S. IPO pegging its $6B valuation on that of Yoox Net-a-Porter.

The comparison of Farfetch and Net-A-Porter makes sense on the surface, but in digging a little deeper, the two companies have very different business models and strategies.

While both Farfetch and Yoox Net-A-Porter offer multi-branded luxe fashion selections, YNAP is a pure e-commerce retailer that controls the entire value chain, from the customer relationship, the product inventory, to fulfillment and the digital presentation of the brands.

By contrast, Farfetch operates as a marketplace, forging partnerships primarily with independent retailers that post selections on the Farfetch marketplace with the retailers handling fulfillment. Once products are sold, Farfetch takes a commission on sales.

To date, Farfetch has created a community between its 2.3 million customers and its nearly 1,000 luxury goods sellers, including 614 retailers and 375 luxury brands.

Farfetch's strategy is to form mutually rewarding partnerships with retailers and brands as a technology leader, both on its global marketplace and through its White Label service supporting **Manolo Blahnik**, **Christopher Kane**, **DKNY**, and **Thom Browne**, among other brands.

Farfetch supports brick-and-morter fashion retail

In this age of Amazon with the demand to create an omni-channel shopping experience, Farfetch doesn't cobble its internet strategies onto an established retail operation. Rather it started in the tech world and uses its digital heft to support the day-to-day operations and sales challenges of brick-and-mortar retailers by bringing the world's fashion shoppers virtually to their door.

"We actually see the future of fashion as centered in the physical store, which I know is ironic for a tech business," said Farfetch CEO and founder José Neves in an interview with *Fast Company*. "We are not a retailer. We are here to help brands and retailers find what the luxury experience is of 2020 and beyond. We want to be the platform for the global fashion industry."

We actually see the future of fashion centered in the physical store.

Farfetch's hook is that experience of discovery that customers find when browsing in a store, but doing it online. London-based Harvey Nichols is the first department store to open its doors on Farfetch, greatly expanding its exposure to luxury shoppers beyond its 15 store locations and its dedicated online shop. Harvey Nichols joins Burberry as major retailers partnering with Farfetch.

Platform business model is the difference

Alex Moazed, founder of Applico and co-author of *Modern Monopolies: How to Dominate in the 21st Century Economy*, explains that at its core Farfetch is not an online fashion retail marketplace, it is platform.

Moazed defines a platform as a business model that "creates value by facilitating exchanges between two or more independent groups, usually consumers and producers. In order to make these exchanges happen, platforms harness and create large scaleable networks of users and resources that can be accessed on demand."

Unlike what Moazed describes as "linear companies," i.e., Macy's, which own the inventory that shows up on its balance sheet, platforms create value by connecting producers and consumers so that meaningful exchanges can be made. "Platforms don't, to use a common phrase, own the means of production – instead, they create the means of connection," he says.

Unlike **Macy's**, which has to buy the stock to fill its 669 stores, Farfetch does not. The 5.7 million SKUs listed in its marketplace this spring and summer, valued at $2.4 billion, are absent from its balance sheet. Farfetch revenues only come once an exchange is made.

"In the 21st century, the supply chain is no longer the central aggregator of business value. What a company owns matters less than what it can connect," Moazed explains.

Platforms are a business model that brings together the makers of goods and consumers. In Moazed's assessment many technology companies, like HBO or Netflix, are linear not platform businesses. Each owns or licenses its content.

"Platform design isn't just about creating the underlying technology. It's about understanding and creating the whole business and how it will create value for and build a network," he advises.

By understanding the underlying platform business model through which Farfetch operates, it is not far-fetched to compare it to other hugely successful platform businesses like Google, Apple, Facebook, and Uber, and in the product marketplace Amazon, eBay, and Etsy.

While Farfetch is often compared to Richemont's Yoox Net-a-Porter, Moazed says that comparison doesn't hold. "The irony is that Farfetch has a truly unique platform business model. Yoox is much more a linear business buying inventory, putting it onto its balance sheet and then being a reseller rather than a pure platform model like Farfetch."

Better late than never

With platforms being the business model of the 21st century, Moazed believes big, traditional linear companies need to wake up to the new business reality.

"The traditional fashion industry hasn't gotten to the point where they understand this asset-light inventory model, but it will ultimately change how they design new product lines," he says, stressing that fashion houses won't have the luxury of producing full-product ranges, filled with losers and a few winners.

"In the past fashion brands could force their retailers to buy their full line so they could get access to the really hot marque items. Platforms do away with that."

Nike understands this as it just did a deal with **StockX,** a sneaker platform marketplace that started with inventory from retailers of high-end sneakers. Now StockX customers can get the latest LeBron Nikes there and trade out older models.

Luxury of Authenticity

Today we live in an age of authenticity. Authentic brands, authentic communications and authentic relationships with consumers is demanded. An overwhelming 86 percent of consumers say brand authenticity is important when deciding which brands to support, according to a study conducted by Stackla.

These findings were validated by another global study by Cohn & Wolfe. In that survey of 15,000 respondents, 91 percent of global consumers said they would reward a brand for its authenticity via "purchase, investment, endorsement or similar action." Of this 91 percent, over 60 percent will either "purchase or express increased purchase interest" in a brand they perceive to be authentic.

Authenticity is the ultimate challenge for luxury brands.

Nowhere in business are the authenticity stakes higher than in the luxury market, where consumers' trust in heritage, craftsmanship, and quality is rewarded by their willingness to pay a premium for the privilege of ownership.

Authenticity is called the ultimate challenge for luxury brands and never has it been more important than for young HENRYs.

"Authenticity is considered the challenge for the luxury segment of our time," write Patricia Anna Hitzler and Günter Müller-Stewens of the University of St. Gallen, Switzerland, in a study entitled "The Strategic

Role of Authenticity in the Luxury Business." In this study, the authors define the primary drivers of luxury brand authenticity to be craftsmanship, scarcity of supply, unique aesthetics and link to origin.

Further, Hitlzer and Müller-Stewens advise that profits must take a back seat to more lasting values and ideals for a truly authentic luxury brand status to be earned.

Inspirational, not aspirational luxury

HENRYs want luxury that is real and meaningful, yet personal and not mass produced. Authenticity is a brand value highly prized by HENRYs, but when they dig a little deeper into the authenticity of many luxury brands – **Louis Vuitton, Prada, Dior** – they find them heavy on marketing, but light on authenticity.

For example, in 2018 Louis Vuitton spent 42 percent of the money it took in – $5.4 billion out of a total $12.9 billion in revenues – on advertising and promotion. By contrast, **Hermès**, a renowned authentic luxury brand but one which is priced beyond the means of most HENRYs, invested only 5 percent of its $6 billion in revenues on advertising, according to Forbes World's Most Valuable Brands list.

Rather than mass-produced, in name-only luxury products, HENRYs crave the real thing.

Too many brands think authenticity is a marketing tactic, not a reality of what the brand is, what it expresses, and what it is affixed to as a product or service.

CASE STUDY: Beekman 1802

Beekman 1802 rejects the 'Lifestyle' label, in favor of 'Living' brand

Michael Kors is doing it. Fashion accessories company **Vera Bradley** and bridal designer **Vera Wang** too. All are trying to create a 'lifestyle' brand. But it sounds contrived and artificial.

That's why Josh Kilmer-Purcell and Dr. Brent Ridge, founders of **Beekman 1802**, reject the 'lifestyle' brand label. It simply doesn't ring true. "We think of ours as a 'living brand.' Everything we put out there is inspired by the life we are living," Ridge said.

Beekman 1802, which makes farm-healthy beauty, food, home, and garden products, announced in 2018 that it was leaving the Evine television shopping network for HSN. It launched at midnight on July 31 and became the biggest launch for a beauty brand in the 41 year history of the company, Ridge told me, adding "and they carry some pretty well-known beauty brands." The first products on deck were its collection of farm-to-skin beauty and Happy Place natural home cleansing products.

More than a business decision

As important as this move is for growing the Beekman 1802 brand, with HSN being five times as large as Evine, Ridge explains the ultimate decision was driven by their personal need to spend more time back on their 60-acre farm in Sharon Springs, New York.

"Our company is dependent upon us drawing

inspiration from our life on the farm. To do that we have to be on the farm," Ridge shared with me. "As we became bigger and bigger on Evine, they wanted us to spend more and more time there. So by going to HSN we are able to commit to just one visit a month and still meet as many new neighbors as we did working with Evine. But it allows us to spend more quality time on the farm."

The farm is both the life-giving force and the heart and soul of Beekman 1802, which spans products, brick-and-mortar retail in Beekman 1802 Mercantile, e-commerce, wholesale distribution through specialty boutiques, licensing partnerships with companies like Target and Bloomingdale's, and publishing. Besides being an accomplished advertising executive, Kilmer-Purcell is also a *New York Times* best-selling author.

"We are authentic to what we are doing," Ridge adds. "It requires us to do the work on the farm to create the products. If we aren't doing those things, then our creative inspiration dries up. We have to be very protective of that source of inspiration."

Bringing neighbor-centricity to HSN

Another essential ingredient in Beekman 1802's success is its neighbors. The company's neighbor-centric philosophy goes back to the very beginnings of the company when its Sharon Springs neighbors taught the founders how to make goats milk soap.

"Our company would never have gotten off the ground if not for our neighbors in Sharon Springs. And our company wouldn't grow without that connection with neighbors who feel they are part of a community," Ridge explains.

Gentlemen farmers make good businessmen

Beekman 1802 was born of necessity back in 2008 when Kilmer-Purcell was working in advertising and Ridge for Martha Stewart Omnimedia both lost their jobs to the recession. They retreated to the farm, which they originally bought as a weekend getaway, and had to figure out how to keep it and themselves going. Making and selling goat-milk soap was the logical answer, as the farm was already home to a herd of goats.

Even as the company expands, everything about the brand speaks to authenticity.

From that single product, a whole range of offerings followed with the goal to help its over 300,000 neighbors "cultivate a better life." Part of that evolution was a line of skincare products with Dr. Ridge applying his medical background to the science and Kilmer-Purcell his advertising expertise to introduce skincare for all in gender-neutral packaging that men especially will feel comfortable having on their bathroom counter.

"When you get down to it, men and women's skin isn't different. We speak on behalf of all skin. It is the modern way to think of skincare," Ridge explains.

Even as the company expands from its flagship goat-milk beauty products into food with **Target** under its Beekman 1802 Farm Pantry line, to home furnishings with **Bloomingdale's**, everything about the brand speaks to authenticity. They are hands-on in everything that they produce and sell, and actively engaged in all aspects of manufacture and marketing what they sell.

They live it, their brand reflects it, and they invite their 'neighbors' to join them in their living-brand experience too.

Gently-Used Luxury

The resale market for fashion is particularly hot. **thredUP**, an online reseller of mass-fashion brands predicts the total resale retail market to reach $41 billion in 2022.

Further the latest Census report on the retail market identifies used-merchandise stores among the fastest-growing sectors this year, up 7.6 percent through the first half of 2018 following an 11.6 percent gain in 2017. And that number doesn't even include online sellers like Thredup and The RealReal.

CASE STUDY: The RealReal

The RealReal Makes the Real Thing Affordable for HENRYs

Long dismissed as an opportunistic upstart of little consequence by the luxury establishment, **The RealReal** is proving it is on to something big. Gently-used luxury fashion is a real trend and The RealReal has discovered the secret sauce: become a trusted and authoritative partner for luxury-fashion consigners and buyers, many of whom are the same person.

In 2017 Julie Wainwright, founder of The RealReal, told CNBC that sales had topped $500 million in the first six years after doing $10 million its first year in 2011. To date, the company has raised $288 million in funding, according to Crunchbase.

The RealReal becomes real

The RealReal got its start online, but like so many other digitally native companies, it is now expanding into brick-and-mortar retail with two permanent locations where luxury consigners and customers can congregate.

One store is located in New York City's SoHo neighborhood and another just opened on Los Angeles' Melrose Avenue close to the Nordstrom Local concept store and Glossier, another digitally native beauty company.

Unique to the new Los Angeles location is a section devoted to men's fashion, a rapidly growing segment of The RealReal's business. It also continues to test opportunities in physical retail through opportunistic pop-up shops, in places like Las Vegas and San Francisco.

Wainwright told me that the stores fill a need for the business that its online presence can't match. The average order size in The RealReal stores are two times larger than online and it is a way to secure the best-quality consignments.

"It is a marketing tactic, sales tactic and product acquisition tactic," Wainwright says. "We find we get lots of high-quality consignments when we do pop-ups."

The RealReal's appeal

For many older affluent consumers, shopping secondhand has been a well-kept secret, something they do on the sly. "Some of the smartest people I know have been buying consignment forever but never talked about it – even some of the richest people I know, because they like good value," Wainwright told CNBC.

But young HENRYs have no such qualms. They love the treasure-hunt experience that only secondhand shopping gives them.

American shoppers are inundated with too much of the same-old, same-old fashion that results in them looking like everyone else. Millennials, most especially, want a look that is all their own, and The RealReal helps them get that.

"Layering, mixing patterns and pairing luxury with contemporary, formal with casual are what's happening now," says Rati Levesque, chief merchant at The RealReal. "It's very individualistic, customizable and authentic."

The RealReal delivers that and at a price, though hardly cheap, that opens the door to luxury that more people can afford. "Americans are value shoppers more than anything," Wainwright says.

"So we find they buy from our site and buy new and

then consign things they may have kept for a couple of months. Then they use the money from consignments to buy new or buy from us again."

What drives them all to The RealReal is a passion for fashion. "Whether someone is a collector, archivist or simply loves fashion, they see something on the site that they remember on the cover of Vogue, or who wore it on the runway, and they have to buy it," explains Levesque. "Often new trends take time to catch on and by the time you're lusting for it, the item may have sold out in the boutique."

"Customers love shopping on The RealReal to find treasures that slipped through their hands or that they never had the opportunity to own before," he continues.

What's hot, what's not

What The RealReal recognizes, and the luxury brands may yet have to learn, is that its resale market is a vital part of the greater luxury market infrastructure. It helps support first-time sales.

"Whenever we survey our consigners or buyers, they say they check out our site before they buy new. It helps them if they are going to spend a lot of money to know that the value is good. Even if they have never consigned, they want to know they can," Wainwright says. "People can't underestimate how smart shoppers are."

"If you know you can make 80 percent of [the price of] an item back, you are more likely to go ahead and make the purchase in the primary market," Levesque adds.

Because luxury fashion trends track in tandem both in the primary and secondary luxury market, The RealReal's new "State of Luxury Resale" report gives a valuable perspective on what luxury fashionistas crave now.

Backed by data on 8 million items sold, The RealReal reports that **Gucci** has pushed **Chanel** aside as the No. 1 brand searched on the site, while **Louis Vuitton** continues as the second-most-searched-for brand, followed by Chanel.

In sales Gucci is the fastest growing, up 62 percent year-on-year, followed by **Hermès**, +40 percent, and Chanel, +34 percent. Of note, Hermès is reported to be the fastest-growing brand among Millennials, up 71 percent among shoppers aged 18 to 34.

People can't underestimate how smart shoppers are.

Regarding this year's fashion trends, Levesque says logo-mania is back. "Iconic, logo-centric styles, notably **Dior**, Gucci and **Fendi**, are coming on strong in resale value, while past-season's styles without 'in-your-face' labels are on the decline."

For men The RealReal is tracking a trend toward casual street styles, with Kanye West's **Yeezy** X Adidas the sneaker of the moment across most of the country. Along with streetwear, The RealReal is also seeing a trend for what it calls "dad-style." Hawaiian shirts are hot (cool), as are "dad" ball caps and fanny packs.

Tracking The RealReal

Online The RealReal is dramatically increasing its traffic this year, according to data compiled by SimilarWeb. "Over the past 18 months, U.S. desktop & mobile web traffic to therealreal.com averages 2.2 million visits per month. This number is up nearly one-third, increasing from an average of 1.9 million visits in the first half of 2017 to 2.5 million in the first half of 2018," says Liron Hakim-Bobrov, Marketing Insights Manager.

"Beyond more traffic, the really important news is that The RealReal visitors are highly engaged, averaging ten pages per visit and bouncing off just 35 percent of the time," she continues.

In another measure of engagement, The RealReal's online visitors know what they are looking for, with nearly half of its website traffic arriving after people type the URL in their search bar and an additional 22 percent coming from organic search. "The RealReal doesn't have to pay to get people to visit," Hakim-Bobrov says, noting only about 8 percent of traffic is from paid search.

Demographically The RealReal's visitors skew toward the Millennial generation's affluents and up-and-comers, with nearly one-third of its traffic coming from people aged 24 to 34, and another 18 percent on each side of them, aged 18 to 23 and 35 to 44.

Having been in the luxury business for the last seven years, The RealReal has a long enough track record to have seen the shift in generations. The trailing edge of the GenXers were 38 then, and the leading edge of the Millennial generation is 38 now.

Millennials, aged 18 to 38, with their taste for luxury and their willingness to search high and low for it, are the key to The RealReal's past and future success. As Wainwright reminds us, "Never underestimate how sharp Millennials are."

Luxury of Access

Atlantic magazine profiled the changing psychology in today's young HENRYs away from the idea of ownership toward access as needed. They write:

> "The emergence of the "sharing economy" – services that use the web to let companies and families share otherwise idle goods – is headlined by **Zipcar**, but it also involves companies such as **Airbnb**, a shared marketplace for bedrooms and other accommodations for travelers; and **thredUP**, a site where parents can buy and sell kids' used clothing."

From a distance, the sharing of cars, rooms, and clothes may seem a curiosity, more hippie than revolutionary. But technology is allowing these practices to go mainstream, and that represents a big new step for consumers.

For decades, inventory management was largely the

province of companies, not individuals, and continual efforts to reduce inventory – the stock of things just sitting around – helped companies improve their bottom line.

But today, peer-to-peer software and mobile technology allow us all to have access, just when we need it, to the things we used to have to buy and hold. And the most powerful application is for cars.

Young people value "access over ownership," says Sheryl Connelly, head of global consumer trends at Ford. "I don't think car-buying for Millennials will ever be what it was for Boomers."

Young people value access over ownership.

Connelly points to Zipcar as the prime example. Zipcars are available whenever they are needed and are a prime example of the sharing economy at work. It's a driving solution for urban dwellers – cars only when you need them. HENRYs can drive cars by the hour or day, with gas and insurance included. It saves hundreds over car ownership, with memberships starting as low as $6 per month. It also offers luxury styles like **Audi**, **BMW**, and **Cadillac**.

In fashion, **Rent the Runway** gives HENRYs access to designer fashion, if and when its needed. Not only can HENRYs rent one outfit for a special need, Rent the Runway now offers an unlimited subscription services where subscribers gain access to three rental items at a time for $139 per month. All access to Rent the Runway fashions is included.

Subscribers select 3 different pieces to keep as long as they want, then they can send 1, 2 or all 3 back and replace them with new pieces. The service comes with insurance to cover minor mishaps and normal wear and tear, though significant damage or lost pieces are billed up to 70 percent of the retail price. Subscribers can cancel the service any time.

Rent the Runway is targeted towards young HENRYs–women who know and love high fashion; want to look glamorous; and experiment with brands without commitment.

➲ OPPORTUNITY: Delayed Gratification

Why instant gratification isn't so gratifying

Ask shoppers what they want and you'll find they want it all – good quality products, wide selection, low prices – and they want it all now. That is the reason that **Amazon** gives every other retailer fits because in the first of those three wants, Amazon pretty well beats all comers.

On the last, instant gratification, Amazon still has a way to go, though the time efficiency of Amazon at the front end when ordering often makes up for any lag in the back end for delivery. Its engineering and fulfillment departments are working overtime to figure out how to make near-instant delivery a reality.

Consumers are driving the demand for instant

gratification, so much so that we are becoming an instant gratification society. Digital marketer Neil Patel says, "Instant gratification is the desire to experience pleasure or fulfillment without delay or deferment. Basically, it's when you want it; and you want it now."

In consumers' quest for "instant gratification" there are two components: the "Instant" now and the "Gratification" from pleasure and fulfillment achieved that leads to personal happiness. But human psychology programs us so that to get the later (i.e., our gratification), we have to give up the former (i.e., the instant). In other words, instant gratification isn't so gratifying.

Your mother told you that anything worth having is worth waiting for. And she was right. Marketers that cater to the truly rich, such as bespoke tailors and shoe markers, artists, jewelers, interior designers and even Hermès with its famed waiting list, understand this essential truth.

As retailers and marketers, it is critical that we separate what consumers say they want from what they really are in search of. When people buy things they don't strictly need, specifically discretionary purchases, which account for at least 70 to 80 percent of all retail, their consuming desire is to achieve greater personal fulfillment and happiness.

They make that purchase, whether a new iPhone, a pair of shoes, watch, handbag, piece of furniture, art for the wall, whatever, because they believe that item will make a meaningful difference in the quality of their lives, i.e., greater happiness.

In a culture as materially rich as ours, shopping is driven primarily by emotional, not physical needs. Yet too few retailers and brands really understand how to play to those emotions, since selling them things is what they have been trained for and always have done.

Luxury marketers are in the happiness business

Despite a long-held belief, retail today is primarily a people, not a product, business. Rather than just selling people products, we ultimately need to focus on fulfilling their emotional desires. That will result in greater happiness for our customers and ultimately greater business success.

To understand our real goal of delivering customer happiness, we need to look at the psychological and behavioral sciences for direction. Fortunately, Dan Clay and John Marshall, members of the innovation team at Lippincott, a global creative consultancy and subsidiary of Marsh & McLennan Companies, have done the work for us in a new report "The Happiness Halo."

Their premise: "Appeal to customers' reason and they're yours for a day. Appeal to customers' emotions and they're yours for a lifetime." To do that, they identify three stages in the customers' path to purchase when retailers and brands have the ability to emotionally impact their customers' lives. "Happiness is as much about how we look forward to [anticipation] and look back on an event [afterglow] as it is the event itself [interaction]."

Clay and Marshall place equal emphasis on each of these stages – anticipation, interaction and afterglow

– and provide strategies for brands to engage emotionally with customers along the way. However, I think the most crucial stage in the Happiness Halo is in customers' anticipation of greater happiness to come. They write, "Positive expectations influence a person's overall happiness as much as actual experiences," citing research by Robb B. Rutledge, et. al., out of University College London. I would amend that statement to say "more influence" based on other research.

Appeal to customers' reason and they're yours for a day. Appeal to their emotions and they're yours for a lifetime.

Professor Marsha Richins, University of Missouri, conducted a comprehensive study of how consumers' expectations influence their ultimate satisfaction with a material goods purchase.

Entitled "When Wanting is Better that Having," Richins found, "Positive emotions were strongest before the purchase was made, as respondents thought about acquiring and using the product. This hedonic elevation was more pronounced for higher-cost goods." In simple English, people were happier as they anticipated a purchase, with their happiness levels declining during and after the purchase was made. In particular, their joy, excitement and contentment peaked before their purchase.

This finding was mirrored by researcher Jeroen Nawijn

in a study entitled "Happiness is . . . looking forward to your vacation." People's vacation happiness peaks during the eight-week period before their holiday experience rather than afterwards. While Nawijn studied vacations specifically, there is no reason to assume it doesn't apply to other purchases, particularly higher-ticket expenditures that take some planning and consideration, like that for a luxury good.

People's imagination is tantalized and their excitement and engagement grow in anticipating the purchase experience to come. That pre-purchase anticipation is a big part of the total customer experience. Retailers and brands will benefit by building it, heightening it and extending it with the result that greater, not lesser, customer satisfaction results.

People's imaginations are tantalized in anticipating the purchase to come.

In effect, how brands and retailers "set the table" for the purchase experience to come yields a more satisfied, gratified and happier customer. That is exactly what Brian Wansink, former Professor and Director of the famed Cornell University Food and Brand Lab, discovered in a study of how people's expectations of a dining experience affect their ultimate satisfaction.

In the experiment, his group served the exact same food to two different groups. One group was served the meal in typical fast-food fashion and the other was presented the same food in a fine dining setting. The only difference between the two groups was how the food was presented and served, not what the food was. The result: the fast-food dining group rated the food they were served 3 points on a 10-point scale. The fine dining group rated the food 8.4 points on the same scale.

The food, its taste and texture (i.e., the product) was exactly the same, what differed were the diners' expectations which were elevated for the fine dining group. Those elevated expectations resulted in much higher overall satisfaction from the experience. They were more gratified.

Instant gratification denies customers an anticipation experience

Retailers' and brands' greatest opportunity today is to get out in front of the customers' experience and help them anticipate an exciting experience to unfold through the purchase and enjoyment of that purchase. Instant gratification strips that anticipatory experience from them. As a result, their overall happiness with their purchase, the interaction, and the afterglow can be compromised.

In "The Happiness Halo" report, Clay and Marshall offer these suggestions to enhance customers' anticipation to more positively impact customers' emotions throughout the interaction and afterglow stages of purchase.

- **Tease – What can your brand hide to build excitement during anticipation?**

Humans are "hard-wired to prioritize 'seeking' over 'finding,'" so the searching and waiting for something wonderful to buy is often more rewarding than actually buying it. This explains consumers' extensive pursuit of pre-purchase research, a phenomenon I have observed often in research with consumers, even as they complain about leading hectic, time-crunched lives. That time spent researching and planning a purchase is rewarding in and of itself.

Another tease that builds anticipation is the waiting list like Apple did for the new iPhones it unveiled in September 2018. Consumers had to wait until mid-October to pre-order their new X phones, while they could immediately pre-order the lower-cost iPhone 8 and 8 Plus. But no matter which phone they wanted, they still had the tease of a wait after their pre-order.

Tempt – What can your brand expose to give customers something to look forward to?

Research shows that people tend to develop a preference for things merely because they are familiar with them – like the new Apple iPhones and how masterfully the company manages the introduction of their new products. It also explains the stage craft designed into runway fashion shows.

Every weekend at **Costco** you can see brands tempting shoppers through sampling. **BMW** offers its famed driving school, not just for brand owners but to tempt potential buyers by experiencing first-hand the handling excellence of the cars. And Apple is working the tease and tempt simultaneously with the new iPhones, as *Business Insider* reports the pre-orders of iPhone 8 were low as people waited to see it and the iPhone X side-by-side.

- **Make it a treat – What moments of your brand experience might be a limited-time treat for customers, and how can you frame them that way?**

Author Robert Cialdini in his book *Influence:The Psychology of Persuasion* writes "Everything's more attractive when availability is limited," think seasonal treats like **Starbucks** Pumpkin Spice Latte, **Samuel Adams** OctoberFest beer, **Cadbury Crème** Eggs, and Girl Scout cookies.

Ubiquity of a luxury product is death for a luxury brand.

Limited editions of a particular item greatly enhance its appeal. It's an essential part of the luxury branding equation since ubiquity of a luxury product is death for a luxury brand. Luxury goods have got to be limited to be special and worth the premium a customer will pay.

In conclusion, while consumers say and believe that they want what they want when they want it, brands that cave to their demands for instant gratification may be doing their customers, and ultimately their brands, a disservice by stripping away the customers' emotional anticipation for something wonderful to come.

Enhancing the emotional reward for customers, not

simply satisfying their perceived physical need for a product, is how retailers and brands can capture that customer for a lifetime, as Maya Angelou reminds us, "People will forget what you said, people will forget what you did, but people will never forget how you made them feel."

Anti-Status Luxury

Consistently in my research with luxury consumers, I have found men more predisposed than women to luxury purchases. They typically spend more on luxury goods and services than women in Unity Marketing surveys and are more willing to express interest in luxury consumption in interviews and other qualitative research.

I've attributed these gender differences in luxury purchasing to the fact that women often manage the household finances and so are more aware of how far the budget must stretch across the monthly fixed and discretionary purchases. That makes women more practical when considering and making luxury purchases.

My research has found men, on the other hand, more indulgent and generally more willing to express interest in luxury purchases. That doesn't mean women don't desire luxuries too, but they may be less willing to admit it.

A new study led by Gideon Nave, assistant professor of marketing at the Wharton School with a specialty in neuroeconomics, suggests that these gender differences in luxury consumption are in the genes, or more precisely in how much testosterone is coursing through the blood stream. The study was published in the latest issue of *Nature Communications*.

High-T men prefer high-status brands

In two controlled double-blind experiments, Nave and his team administered doses of testosterone to one group of men with another group given a placebo. Then each group was asked to rank a set of brands that had in pre-testing before testosterone was introduced been equally matched as to perceived quality but with one brand ranked higher in prestige or status value.

The results of this first test found that men with elevated testosterone levels preferred higher-status brands, for example high-prestige **Calvin Klein** Jeans versus low-status **Levi's**. Both brands, however, were rated as being equal in quality.

The second test tried to tease apart men's perception of brands' status from their quality and power-enhancing values. Nave explained the importance of this, "We were trying to disentangle power from status. Typically in the animal kingdom they go together, but you can think of examples in human society where they don't," he said. "A border patrol agent has lots of power but not status. And a famous climate scientist may have a lot of status but little power."

What do millennial HENRYs Want?

In this test testosterone-treated and placebo-administered men were asked to review mock ads for six different luxury products with three different positionings: quality, power, and prestige. In this test, too, men with the elevated levels of testosterone exhibited preference for high-status brands. Brands tested were **Alpina** watches, **Audi** cars, **Mont Blanc** pens, **Keurig** coffeemakers, **Urbanears** ear phones, and **Ray-Ban** sunglasses.

For example, the Ray-Ban quality-positioned ad highlighted the sun glasses "excellent quality, lightness, durability and comfort." The power positioning called out Ray-Ban Aviator Classics as "designed for U.S. commando warriors in combat," and stressed the glasses' "superior visual clarity, high performance materials and comfort." Ray-Ban's prestige ad focused on its "superior style and cachet," and described the glasses as being "iconic, timeless frames." All three ads ended with a statement that reinforced the brand's quality, i.e., "the polarized lenses provide optimum visual clarity and 100% UV protection."

The study authors concluded, "Our results demonstrate for the first time that T causally influences rank-related consumer preferences and that the effect is driven by status enhancement and not power motives or inclination of high quality." In other words, when it comes to positioning luxury brands for men, status and prestige beat power and quality hands down.

From the lab to the shop floor

A caveat in the research is that the sample size was relatively small, fewer than 250, though the authors note that it is the largest sample in similar studies to date. It was conducted exclusively with men, and while women have small amounts of testosterone, the authors suggest that hormones related to women's menstrual cycles may have an effect. And this study only measured brand preferences, not actual purchases where real money is exchanged to actually achieve higher-personal status.

That said, in marketing perception is reality and building aspiration for a specific brand is critical to the whole idea of luxury marketing. This study provides ample evidence that men with their higher levels of testosterone are more driven to aspire for luxury brands that offer the promise to gain greater social status and prestige. That at least is what high-T men aspire to, more so than achieving personal power or confidence from high-quality purchases.

What is status? That may depend.

What exactly is status and how that is measured on an individual basis may not be as clear-cut as a man choosing to buy a pair of expensive Calvin Klein or more affordable Levi's jeans. My husband, for example, is a Levi's loyalist. I suspect part of the brand's appeal is that his 32" waist size is prominently displayed on the label.

He takes great pride in the fact that having grown into this size in his teens, he has never outgrown them, some 40 years later. That he gains status from how he has controlled his weight and maintained his physique is without question and far more significant than the amount of money in his wallet.

I've heard much the same thing from young men in research. Their status is derived from who they are and what they have achieved, not by the particular expensive brands they buy. One young man on a career path leading to affluence explained that his status came from the initials after his name, in his case PhD, not which brands he bought.

For HENRYs status is derived from who they are and what they have achieved, not by the particular expensive brands they buy.

Another young associate lawyer talked about how the gray-haired senior partners in his law firm wear expensive **Rolex** or **Patek Philipe** watches. But he said his "status" watch was his $100 **Timex** Ironman because it signaled "who I am – a triathlete. It says 'I need this kind of watch.'" Perhaps his watch brand preferences will change as his salary grows or he gives up triathlons, but today he clearly derives status from what he does and who he is, not the brands he wears.

My research leads me to conclude that while status is important to everyone, how each individual measures and expresses his or her personal status may be different, most especially for the millennial generation.

Thorstein Veblen in his seminal work, *The Theory of the Luxury Class*, published in 1899 described luxuries as "positional goods," which signal status through economic (e.g., high price) or physical (e.g., limited access) barriers. As a result, wealthy people are drawn to luxury "positional goods" that proclaim one's higher status, thus distinguishing themselves from the lower-status masses who are limited to more affordable and accessible goods.

Luxury on the inside, not on the outside

The Millennial generation may challenge Veblen's theory of conspicuous consumption. While there are still economic limitations to some luxury goods, the rising tide of wealth is breaking down those barriers. And the status value of exclusivity is almost meaningless in today's digital economy with access to luxuries at millennials' fingertips.

Millennial HENRYs and those on the road to affluence generally reject the old assumptions of conspicuous consumption where purchasing luxury brands confers greater social status, in favor of more conscientious consumption where purchases are made based on values inherent in the brands and to the individual. As a result, they look inside themselves and the brands they consider buying for meaningful value, not to the outside and what others may think about them from the brands they wear, cars they drive, or how they furnish their homes.

Of course, luxury brands self select their customers through marketing and positioning. Some people may be attracted to brands that offer a higher-status value on the outside, as Nave's research shows.

But I suspect among the next generation of luxury consumers, these external prestige and social-status markers will play less and less of a role in luxury purchasing, replaced by a more enlightened new-luxury style that is more subtle, less elitist and inherently values driven. For millennials it is more about luxury on the inside than on the outside.

CASE STUDY: Jeep

Jeep understands HENRYs

Jeep is a brand steeped in history. Jeep is the vehicle that won World War II, or at the very least ferried all the generals and officers who won that war. It's been on every other battle field since then and had a starring role in war movies and television series that drove it full speed ahead into the popular culture.

Jeep is as American as apple pie. It is rugged, reliable, resilient and dependable. It gets the job done. Jeep is a brand that proudly waves that flag.

Unlike Mercedes or GM which are much broader based companies with a wider range of brands, the narrower range of Jeep brands share a common DNA: authenticity. All the models in the Jeep portfolio share that DNA:

Jeep Cherokee	Starting at $24,000	SUV
Jeep Grand Cherokee	$30,000	Luxury SUV
Jeep Compass	$21,000	Compact SUV
Jeep Renegade	$18,000	Compact SUV
Jeep Wrangler	$24,000	Classic and most popular
Jeep Wrangler Unlimited	$28,000	Luxury Classic

Today the brand is owned by Fiat Chrysler Automobiles. A recent report from carsalesbase.com reveals that Wrangler sales have grown from almost 81,000 vehicles in 1997 to roughly 191,000 vehicles in 2017. Jeep sales in the first five months of 2018 (more than 110,000 vehicles) are outpacing sales during the first five months of 2015 – the landmark year for total units sold (almost 203,000 vehicles).

Whose buying all those Jeeps?

SBI's Pat Breman, senior consultant, recently did a deep dive into the psychological makeup of the Jeep brands using her company's VALS™ study which has identified 8 distinctive types of personalities of consumers that describe how an individual will express himself or herself as a consumer.

When it comes to car buying in general, and Jeep brands in particular, Breman says you only need to look to three VALS™ types:

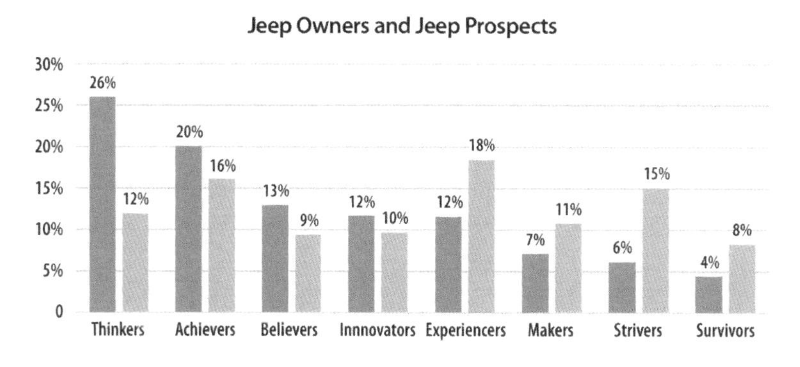

> "When it comes to vehicles, it is down to the point where only three groups that are buying anything: Thinkers, Achievers, and Innovators. What they are buying is different, but they are the only ones that can afford anything these days. Experiencers have the interest, they just don't yet have the money. But the other three groups do."

In addition, while Believers may own a Jeep, because of limited resources, they are more likely to own an older model, not be in the running to buy a new car.

What they all share – Thinkers, Achievers and Innovators – is average income over $100,000, i.e., HENRYs. Experiencers, on the other hand, may report high household income, but because of their age, they are more likely to be reporting the HHI of their parent's not themselves. "Many Experiencers are still living in their parents' basement," Breman shares.

For all, the appeal of Jeep is that it isn't a run-of-the-mill or cookie-cutter SUV. Jeeps have a distinctive look. Jeep offered authentic sport utility vehicles before anyone heard the term SUV.

"It is not their parent's SUV. Some people want to be distinctive and don't have a lot of options to do so especially if they are constrained by money," Breman says, and adds, "These cars are very distinctive without being weird. Jeep isn't weird looking. It is authentic."

Thinkers want reliability

Of all the VALS types, Thinkers have the highest level of Jeep ownership. Thinkers are attracted to brands like Jeep that are safe and conservative, practical and durable and responsible. "They run all the numbers. They do all the research. They can tell you more about a vehicle than the sales person on the floor at the dealership," Breman explains.

> "They may not be buying the Wrangler, and may gravitate toward more expensive Cherokee models – think Wrangler for mature adults. The history of the brand is attractive to Thinkers. Jeep's decades-long track record proves the brand's durability and reliability."

What is interesting in the data, however, is that there is a gap between Thinker ownership (26 percent) and Thinker willingness to buy a Jeep (12 percent). Given their propensity to delve into the data before making a purchase, Thinkers may be finding the newer Jeep models aren't measuring up or that other brands such as Subaru fill the safety and reliability niche better.

Jeep is not their parents' SUV.

This can have implications for how Jeep is presenting itself to the Thinker audience. For Thinkers, marketing that focuses on quality, reliability and longevity is called for, rather than marketing with a more lifestyle focus.

Achievers want to show

"Achievers have a 'me-first, my family-first' attitude." Breman says. These consumers are likely to have children, and will look to Jeep Grand Cherokee model to do the hauling. On the other hand, they might buy a Wrangler as their teenager's car. "Typically they see money as defining success. So they might own a luxury car and a Jeep as well, because Jeep isn't necessarily a 'prestige' brand. But it has badge value that communicates a strong message about who they are: hard working, like their Jeep."

Innovators want authenticity

Of the VALS types, Innovators have the highest incomes. More importantly, Innovators are confident enough to experiment; they tend to view advertising with skepticism. For them, they want the real deal. "Innovators are, number one, into authenticity," Breman says. "They are also into experiences, but not the typical tourist experience like a cruise or tour to Europe. They want different experiences, like a trip up the Amazon or to go hiking in the Himalayas. Jeep's off-roading capability can be a turn on."

Innovators are independent by nature. The Wrangler or the Unlimited will have appeal to Innovators who don't want to run with the pack, but chart their own course.

Experiencers can't wait

Experiencers have the greatest aspiration for the Jeep brand among all the VALS types, with 18 percent saying they would buy a Jeep. But as of yet, most Experiencers haven't yet fulfilled that aspiration. "As the youngest of the types, Experiencers are dynamic, always on the go. They want the Jeep experience, but for most, their incomes haven't caught up to their appetites," Breman explains.

Experiencers want to find their own path. "Jeep pretty much says I am an independent person. Plus Jeep has the macho factor going for it, with a don't-mess-with-me-look to its grill," she continues.

While the Wrangler is picture perfect for Experiencers, because of their modest incomes, they may lean toward Jeep's entry-level Renegade model.

Jeep's brand promise: Freedom, Adventure, Authenticity, Passion

As a brand, Jeep defines its promise as "Vehicles enabling life's extraordinary journeys." It explains its goal to: "Provide vehicles that support a lifestyle of boundless freedom, responsible adventure, and are reliable, safe, fun and environmentally friendly."

Jeep is an experiential brand that most especially takes its owners outdoors, rather than to the grocery store or mall. And, in that the VALS types have distinctly different approaches to outdoor experiences. Thinkers, for example, are more likely to go outdoors because nature provides them a place to rejuvenate and renew. Achievers go outdoors because it is a place to engage in activities with their children. Innovators often go to the outdoors to enjoy or explore its aesthetics or to engage in a variety of personally challenging activities. And Experiencers, as their name implies, go outdoors to engage in a variety of physically challenging experiences.

HENRYs' experiential turn

Jeep's most engaged consumers now and in the future are the Thinkers, Achievers, Innovators and Experiencers. Breman sees a common thread that motivates them all: The value of intangibles over tangibles.

"When Baby Boomers grew up, it was all about consumerism. That is what made the consumer marketplace grow into what it is today," she says. "But today the value of owning things is being replaced by a desire for experience."

The old adage, "He that dies with the most toys wins," has now been replaced. It now is,"He [or she] that dies with the best toys wins." Jeep understands this shift and is aiming to provide its customers with the best toys with the heritage of Wrangler, its pacesetter.

Marketing to HENRYs

HENRYs demand luxury that speaks to their unique values, namely:

- Luxury that is inclusive, yet individualized (e.g., **Lovesac** Sactionals or **handmadebrogues.com**);
- Luxury that is self-expressive, not self-absorbed or narcissistic (e.g., **TAG Heuer**);
- Luxury that is democratic and not elitist and reserved only for the 1 percent (e.g., **Shinola**);
- Luxury that is authentic and made for them, not some reality television star (e.g., **Canada Goose**);
- Luxury that delivers unique and meaningful experiences (e.g., **Farfetch**); and
- Luxury that is inspirationally authentic, not mass-produced and marketed as aspiration (e.g., **1stdibs**).

Do It Right

Marketing successfully to HENRYs takes new strategies, but some brands already understand the skills involved. Here are some tips to maximize sales by attracting a more affluent audience to boost sales and generate growth:

1. **Be vigilant about service** – Nobody likes to go "slumming" at retail, but some customers are more willing to forgo services in favor of cheap merchandise, or they simply haven't experienced better. HENRYs, on the other hand, may have tasted the high life at retail and know and appreciate high levels of service, including well-maintained merchandise, intelligent displays, and service personnel who know how to make customers feel welcome.

   It is this high level of service that **Costco** does so well, all the while offering sizable and meaningful discounts on premium merchandise. Yes, Costco does little in the way of signage, but every time one steps into a Costco store, the merchandise is well maintained and well organized.

   Further, the service personnel are just delighted to be there and to have you join them in the store. Their cheerful attitude is contagious and powerfully attracts high-potential HENRY customers who can refuse to do business with retailers that populate their stores with surly, unfriendly, or unhelpful staffers.

   Too many marketers make the mistake of thinking that retail is a product business, when in fact it is a people business. Today, customers can find good products virtually anywhere, and now, anytime, thanks to the internet. People go to the store to have an experience and be treated well by other people; it's an incredibly important part of the package.

At the other end of the spectrum is luxury retailer **Nordstrom**, renowned for customer service. Nordstrom succeeds by hitting all the right notes for both the Ultra-affluent and HENRY customers, combining high fashion merchandise across a wide range of price points with attention to the customer's needs that is second to none. As a result, Nordstrom consistently ranks number one among luxury retailers in Unity Marketing's Affluent Consumer Tracking Study (ACTS) for both the Ultra-affluent and the mass-affluent HENRY shoppers.

2. **Showcase quality and workmanship by telling inspiring brand stories** – Luxury marketers are experts about weaving stories around their brands to distinguish their high-priced goods from the ordinary, mass-market offerings. To appeal to HENRYs, marketers must copy strategies from the luxe-branding playbook to set their products apart and above the mass. It can work for just about any product, even the lowly flip-flop.

   Footwear company **Havaianas** uses clever storytelling and trendy design, along with colorful foot beds and slim thong bands to differentiate the product above the generic. They have transformed Havaianas into a luxury flip-flop, yet still highly affordable with prices starting at $16.

But what really sets the brand apart is its attention catching in-store displays featured in its high-end retailing partners' stores, like Saks Fifth Avenue and Bloomingdale's, and its clever use of pop-up shops to create an experience for new customers. The pop-up shops offer customers a chance to create their own flip-flop with design elements including Swarovski crystals to deliver the ultimate luxury flip-flop experience for only $200.

3. **Play to a smart shopper** – Besides income, another demographic that sets HENRYs above the middle income customers is higher levels of education. Overall just about one-third of U.S. households are headed by someone with a college education, but it's double for HENRYs, about two-thirds of whom have a college degree or better. Further, they hold management and executive level jobs which often include budgetary responsibility. They don't leave their business smarts at the office when they go home at night. They are careful money managers, trained to evaluate various purchasing options, and experts at making tradeoffs to achieve the optimum return on investment.

   As mentioned, HENRYs don't go in for status-symbol buying, specifically spending more than they can afford (i.e., a **Rolex** watch) to make a social statement. In recent focus groups, recall that a young HENRY lawyer who shared that his status-symbol watch was his **Timex** Ironman Triathlon, which sends a message of who he is (an athlete) and what he values (practical, down-to-earth items), rather than extravagance and traditional luxury.

In HENRY circles, bragging rights come from getting a good deal, as well as being in the know about smart purchases. The Japan-based global clothing retailer **Uniqlo** has nailed that "smart shopper" cachet. One of its more widely recognized offerings, the $70 Ultra-Light Down Jacket which comes with its own carry pouch, is cool and chic in an anti-status, smart shopper way – a new kind of conscientious consumption in a cultural environment that is demonizing income inequality and the excesses of the 1 percent.

4. **Hit the premium pricing "sweet spot" between mass and class** – HENRYs, when given a choice between the good, better, or best of the best in any product or service category, pick the middle ground. They want something above the standard issue, but not something super exclusive and high priced. The best value by far can be found in the premium level, above the mass-market price, but below the luxury level.

Parachute is a bed linens brand that makes the most of its premium pricing, combined with all the quality features and values of luxury linens. The brand offers high perceived value in its bed linens made with the same high-class Italian cotton as the luxe and super-luxe brands, yet priced for much less than what one might expect to pay for the 'name' brands. As a result, Parachute offers the same Ultra-luxe sleep quality as **Sferra** or **Frette**, but costs a fraction of the price of those brands, with packages starting at $299 for a king-sized set.

Provide an On-Ramp to Luxury

Heritage luxury brands need to provide an on-ramp to their brands for HENRYs. It is not just about pricing right, or pricing down, though that was one of the strategies that **TAG Heuer** used after its effort to move upmarket to the range of $5,000 to $10,000 stalled.

It is about getting the messaging right, as **Gucci** has done thanks to its young creative director, Alessandro Michele, and CEO Marco Bizzarri's hands-off management style that gives Michele free reign to test the brand's boundaries.

Another heritage luxury brand facing the on-ramp challenge is **Yves Saint Laurent**. After its founder's passing, it put the brand under the helm of the next generation design directors, first with Hedi Slimane, and now Anthony Vaccarello (36 years old).

These young designers have found a way to tell a new authentic story for today and reinvent this heritage luxury brand for tomorrow. HENRYs are looking to brands and shopping experiences that capture their unique mood and spirit. They want brands that are authentic and for today, not yesterday.

By dropping the Yves from the brand name, but keeping **Saint Laurent Paris**, it connects to the brand's past, but looks forward to the future.

While some of the Saint Laurent fashions feature glitz and glam, there is a minimalist, back-to-basics aesthetic, especially among the menswear designs, that connects with the current mood.

Vaccarello is honoring the YSL-edge, but telling a new story reinterpreted and made authentic for today's hipsters.

Change Is Coming and HENRYs Are the Change Agents

Bain & Company is the world's authority on the luxury market, tracking industry sales and performance in the personal luxury space. It reports the global luxury market, including both luxury goods and experiences, posted 5 percent growth in 2017 to reach $1.2 trillion globally. After what it calls a "reboot" from 2015–2016, it sees the luxury market reaching a "new normal" of 4 to 5 percent annual growth through 2020.

Taking credit for this exuberant forecast is the rising tide of luxury-leaning Millennials, many of whom start their rise into true affluence as HENRYs, that luxury brands are finally starting to connect with.

"It's an interesting time in the world of luxury – the millennial state of mind has changed the way purchases are made across generations and has pushed luxury brands to redefine what they deliver to customers," said Claudia D'Arpizio, a Bain partner and lead author of the study. "For brands that manage to get this right, there is significant potential growth in the market for personal luxury goods in the years ahead."

In the study, Bain identifies several key trends shaping the luxury market's future. Here's what you need to know to be prepared for the many changes that the young HENRYs will bring to the luxury market as well to every other one:

- **Experi(m)ent(i)al – For "Me" about the Individual**
  Luxury experiences (e.g., hospitality, cruises) and what it terms "experiencing goods" (e.g., food and beverage) are the fastest growing categories in Bain's assessment. Traditional luxury goods, on the other hand, are less relevant to millennials. As a result, personal luxury goods brands are called on to "build story-telling through inspirational conversations and experiences."

  In other words, personal luxury goods brands must transform the things they sell into experiences for these customers. Story-telling, especially through the digital channels where these customers take their cues, is one way to do that, as is offering a chance to "experiment" with the brand through lower-cost offerings, such as beauty, sunglasses, scarves, t-shirts and street wear.

- **Healthier – "New Normal" Return to Growth after Reboot**
  Since 1996, Bain identifies six ages in the personal

luxury market. Throughout those ages of luxury – Sortie Du Temple ('90-'00), Democratization ('01-'07), Crisis ('08-'09), Chinese Shopping Frenzy ('10-'14), Reboot ('15-'16) and now New Normal – only four years have posted a decline in sales.

Though after less than a year, it may be early to identify that the luxury market has crossed over into a new normal state, Bain expects the millennials who make up 38 percent of the luxury consumer market to increase their share of spending (now 30%) to match their penetration over the years ahead.

Another sign of health Bain identifies is that traffic is growing among both luxury market customers and tourists. In the past, tourist spending contributed more heavily in certain global markets, but in the "new normal" period the spending is expected to even out.

Key for optimizing luxury brand growth in today's "new normal" period is to develop one-on-one relationships with the next generation consumers on which their future depends.

Ecosystematic – Evolving Ecosystem of Channels based on Customers

To my mind, this trend toward defining channels of distribution based upon how the customers want to engage with brands, not how the company wants to manage its operations, is one of the most important take-aways in this study. They write, "Channels are now coming together in an interdependent and integrated ecosystem around the customer."

Sageberry Consulting's Steven Dennis, explains that too many brands are substituting omnichannel tactics for customer engagement strategies. Brands, he said, "need to have a well-sequenced roadmap of digital marketing and channel integration initiatives rooted in a deep understanding of customer behavior and underlying economics."

In the evolving omnichannel ecosystem for luxury brands, Bain calls out the complementary roles of retail and wholesale, the need to leverage online as a support platform for all physical channels, travel/airport and off-price retail as a means to widen the customer base with less intimidating ways to explore luxury brands and the vital need for e-commerce engagement.

The latter, e-commerce, remains a sticking point for some luxury brands and perhaps rightly so, for Bain reports online sales represent less than 10 percent of luxury brand sales. But that share is expected to grow to approximately 25 percent by 2025.

With 20,000 luxury mono-branded stores worldwide, brands must manage the omnichannel "network" from human touchpoints to digital engagement. Brands that have been slow to embrace all that digital interaction offers customers, including the purchase option, must see that a complete 360° digital platform is the tipping point to relevance with millennials.

Post-Aspirational – Traditional Market Segmentation Is Losing Relevance

I for one am glad to see the demise of the term "aspirational" to describe millennial HENRYs. It just doesn't apply. Millennials aren't aspiring to join some elite group that is defined by status. They seek to stand out and define themselves as individuals who share common values.

The post-aspirational customer as defined by Bain is distinguished by "being able to make a personal statement" through style and brand choices, not the old luxury concept of exclusivity found by purchasing brands favored by the "happy few."

The post-aspirational consumers are finding ways to express their individuality and engage with luxury brands through new ranges of luxury streetwear offerings relevant to HENRYs more casual lifestyle. These new categories, including sneakers, denim, t-shirts, parkas, down jackets, and rubber slides, make the brands relevant to millennials' casual new-luxury lifestyles, rather than some idealized formal lifestyle that old luxury represents.

Curated – Inspiring Customers through All Touchpoints

Brands need to change the goals of marketing from aspiring to inspiring customers. Bain identifies the retail store as the "epicenter of the brand story-telling." That means high-touch, not high-tech, is the way millennials will truly be inspired, with digital engagement most often concluding with the in-store experience, even as e-commerce will grow. The store, therefore, must be a place for immersion into the brand, where the service experience matches the brand promise and connects with the customer's expectations that the brand has inspired.

Curation goes far beyond curating products for local tastes. It is about curating the brand stories for the specific interests and needs of young HENRYs in search of a place to engage, whether online or in-store.

Polarized, Profitable, Evolving – Economics of Luxury Industry Evolving

As final trend Bain finds, that the luxury industry remains a highly profitable one, but one where revenue and profit growth is becoming more expensive. It predicts that approximately 65 percent of companies would achieve revenue growth in 2017, compared with approximately 50 percent during the "reboot" period from 2015 to 2016. But only about 35 percent of those revenue-growth companies will also achieve profit growth for 2018. It predicts that "Industry P&L [is] shifting increasingly in the next years." The solution Bain recommends is to "invest in people, competencies and become marketing-centered."

In conclusion, Bain & Company produced an important report on the evolving luxury market and the challenges and opportunities therein. But while it distills the market perspective into 40+ pages, it is a complex story of industry change and transition that should be humbling for anyone competing here.

Success for players in the new luxury market will depend upon understanding these macro issues, but interpreting them internally to find unique paths to growth. Rather than focusing on the big picture, luxury leaders need to look at their own house. Is it truly aligned with the needs, expectations and desires of the next generation of customers most especially HENRYs? Does it understand that customer up-close-and-personal, not as a market segment, but as individuals.

Big data gives leaders some of the tools they need to do this, but it provides only one perspective, not the kind of understanding actually meeting and talking to customers and potential customers can give. Being truly market-centered, not industry-, competitor-, or product-centered is the answer.

Final Thoughts

Pillars of New Luxury

As we conclude this deep-dive into the HENRY demographic and how they interpret luxury and integrate it into their lifestyles, it is important to understand just how vital HENRYs are to every brand's future in the high-end luxury market, as well as in every consumer-facing goods and services category.

On an individual basis a HENRY household's spending power is dwarfed by that of the rich-now Ultra-affluent household. But as a group, the 30 million HENRYs combined contribute four-times more than Ultras to the consumer economy.

All told, Ultra-affluents, who make up 4 percent of total U.S. households, only account for 10 percent of total consumer spending. HENRYs, by comparison, comprise roughly 40 percent of total consumer expenditures, leaving the middle-and-lower income households (under $100k annually) making up the other 50 percent of consumer spending.

Distribution of Households by Income and Spending

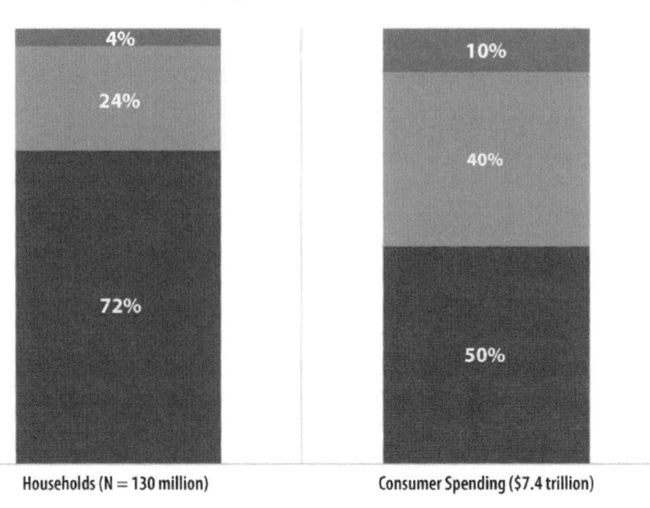

Source: U.S. BLS CEX and Unity Marketing

On average Ultra-affluents spend three-times more than households under $100k and HENRYs spend twice as much. Yet due to their greater numbers, the HENRYs are the customers that every marketer needs. They are even more important to luxury brands because the highest-spending customer in the future starts out as a HENRY today.

Traditional Pillars of Luxury Must Evolve

The traditional pillars of luxury on which so many luxury brands are founded need to evolve as the young HENRYs continue to become the dominant force in the luxury market's future.

Here are the pillars of the new luxury market:

From exclusivity to elusiveness

Exclusivity reeks of elitism and privilege, qualities that repel rather than attract HENRYs. Instead of positioning new luxury brands around the old idea of exclusivity, luxury brands must evolve to being elusive and for that special someone that values that uniqueness.

Limited edition releases, special local offerings and special product releases or experiences grounded in a place and time are all on trend for the HENRY perspective.

From a designers' creative expression to their own

Designers may be the rock stars of traditional luxury, but in the world of new luxury a designers' vision takes second place to the individuals' own.

Rather than taking a designers' endorsement that, "This is what I designed and you need," young HENRYs are looking to be the designer of their lives, their closets and their homes.

They are the curators of their own lifestyle and value new luxury brands that understand that the customer's personal vision is more important than the designer's name on the brand.

Think 'touch of the maker' instead of craftsmanship

Traditional luxury brands make much of their craftsmanship. For HENRYs that craftsmanship must evolve into a more personal and intimate expression of craft.

Maker culture is taking hold among the next generation consumers, which is distinct from the designer culture of traditional luxury brands where the designer is many steps removed from the actual design going out the door.

HENRYs want to know not just that something is made to the highest standards of craftsmanship. They want to know who made it and how they made it, which imparts deeper meaning to the brands they are consider making a part of their lives.

HENRYs want to feel the authentic touch of the maker and see their fingerprints on brand.

From product to experience

Traditional luxury brands have historically led with product, with the experience of shopping and using the product secondary. In new luxury, the priority is reversed. HENRYs think first about the experience that the product will deliver along with the experience of searching out and finding it.

In the new luxury market, brands must turn their "product" into an experience. Apple made its name designing and selling innovative technology products, but senior vice president, Apple retail, Angela Ahrendts describes the Apple Stores as the company's "largest products," because they're now places where people come together to congregate and learn.

This technology giant understands how to turn its products into experiences for its customers.

Heritage and provenance give way to story

Traditional luxury brands make the most of their heritage and provenance. Many of these brands are more than a century old and stay firmly rooted in their history.

HENRYs care less about how long a brand has been around and where it came from. Rather they are concerned with where the brand is today and where it is going tomorrow.

The founding story of a new luxury brand is still important, but less as a badge of honor and more as a reason why the brand is relevant to the customers' real-world concerns and needs today and tomorrow.

HENRYs look to the future and are not so interested in a brand's past. Rather they want to know how the brand fits into their future.

Move over sophistication and aesthetic; For HENRYs it's get back to basics

Traditional luxury brands are elevated by an aesthetic of refined sophistication and elegance that only the chosen few can afford. New luxury goes in the other direction, putting priority on being real.

HENRYs are getting back-to-basics as their

lifestyles get more harried and the culture more complicated. We see their preference for natural origins in the food they eat and the beauty products they use, but their desire for simplicity goes far beyond into all aspects of their lives.

Become a Brand that HENRYs Love

This book is a road map to the future of the luxury market and the consumers who live there – The HENRYs. Acting as your guide, I gave you the sign posts along the way, including a deep-dive into those who have the means to buy luxury, thanks to their high income now with the potential for even higher earnings in the future.

I spotlighted the HENRYs that represent your greatest opportunity, those aged 35 to 54, who are at the prime age for acquiring goods and services to support their lifestyles. And I explained the unique motivations of HENRYs that move them into the market and to buy.

Along the way I called out unique opportunities where white space exists in the new luxury market ready to be filled and gave insight from profiles of new luxury brands that HENRYs love.

Now my work has ended and yours begins. Get out there and meet the HENRYs and make your brand one that they will love. Good "luxe."

Index to Brands

Index to Sources

About the Author

Speaker, author, and market researcher **Pamela N. Danziger** is internationally recognized for her expertise on the world's most influential consumers: the American Affluent, including the HENRYs (high-earners-not-rich-yet) mass affluent.

As founder of Unity Marketing in 1992, Pam leads with research to provide brands with actionable insights into the minds of their most profitable customers. She is also a principal with Retail Rescue, which offers focused and effective consulting, training and mentorship in retail management, marketing, sales and operations.

Pam is a member of the renowned Leaders in Luxury + Design panel recognized by The Home Trust International. She received the Global Luxury Award for top luxury industry achievers presented at the Global Luxury Forum in 2007. She was named to *Luxury Daily*'s Luxury Women to Watch in 2013. She is a member of Jim Blasingame: The Small Business Advocate's Brain Trust and a contributing columnist to *The Robin Report* and *Forbes.com.*

She is the author of nine books including *Putting the Luxe Back in Luxury: How New Consumer Values are Redefining the Way We Market Luxury* (Paramount Market Publishing, 2011); *Let Them Eat Cake: Marketing Luxury to the Masses – as Well as the Classes,* (Dearborn Trade Publishing, 2005) and *Why People Buy Things They Don't Need: Understanding and Predicting Consumer Behavior* (Chicago: Dearborn Trade Publishing, 2004).

A prolific writer and blogger, she focuses on the home and interior design markets with *Marketing the Luxury of Interior Design* (2017) and *Home for HENRYs: Meet the New Customers Home Décor Marketers Are Searching For—High-Earners-Not-Rich-Yet* (Paramount Market Publishing, 2017), as well as retail. In 2016 she added *Shops that POP! 7 Steps to Extraordinary Retail Success* (Paramount Market Publishing, 2016) to her bibliography, which reveals the secrets to crafting a retail shopping experience that's irresistible to high value shoppers.

Among her many television appearances and interviews, she has appeared on the NBC *Today Show,* CBS *News Sunday Morning,* CNN, Fox News, NPR's *Marketplace,* and CNN *In the Money* and was featured in the CNBC special "The Costco Craze: Inside the Warehouse Giant." She is frequently called upon by the *Wall Street Journal, New York Times, Forbes, USA Today, Associated Press, Los Angeles Times, Chicago Tribune, Women's Wear Daily* and other business and consumer publications for commentary and analysis.

As a luxury market expert, Pam is frequently called on to share research-based insights with audiences and business leaders all over the world. She holds a B.A. in English Literature from Pennsylvania State University and a M.L.S. from University of Maryland.